Junior Objects

by Yegor Bugayenko

Copyright © 2020 by Yegor Bugayenko

All rights reserved. No part of the contents of this book may be reproduced or transmitted in any form or by any means without the written permission of the publisher.

Printed and bound in the United States of America.

Version: 1.1
Git hash: 09813ee
Date: September 9, 2020
Words: 36232
Vocabulary: 3833

ISBN: 979-8642988824
Place: Palo Alto, California, USA
Size: 224 pages
Recommended price: $40,96
Web: http://www.yegor256.com/junior-objects.html

✉ book@yegor256.com 🐦 in ⌥ ⌾ f yegor256

Published by Amazon.

"Object-oriented programming is an exceptionally bad idea."

–Edsger W. Dijkstra[1]

---

[1] *TUG LINES*, Issue 32, August 1989.

Contents

Acknowledgements		**9**
Preface		**11**
1	**First**	**13**
	1.1 Hardware	14
	1.2 Software	18
	1.3 File	20
	1.4 Program	25
	1.5 Language	27
	1.6 IDE	30
	1.7 Runtime	32
	1.8 Abstraction	35
	1.9 Maintainability	38
	1.10 Documentation	41
2	**Second**	**49**
	2.1 Indentation	50
	2.2 Console	56
	2.3 Object	59
	2.4 Name	61
	2.5 Visibility	63
	2.6 Variable	65
	2.7 Type	69

2.8	Method	75
2.9	Operator	78
2.10	Statement	80
2.11	Constructor	81
2.12	Attribute	83
2.13	Exception	89

3 Third 95

3.1	Version control	95
3.2	Pull request	100
3.3	Unit test	104
3.4	Mock	108
3.5	Framework	111
3.6	Package	116
3.7	Build	119
3.8	Static analysis	124
3.9	Test coverage	128
3.10	DevOps	130
3.11	Lifecycle	133

4 Fourth 137

4.1	Requirements	138
4.2	Architecture	145
4.3	Design	150
4.4	Refactoring	157
4.5	Integration Test	163
4.6	DRY	168
4.7	Concurrency	171
4.8	Design Patterns	180
4.9	Decorators	190
4.10	Boolean	203
4.11	IoC	204

4.12 Immutability 208

Epilogue   **213**

Index   **217**

Acknowledgements

Many thanks to these guys, who reviewed the book and helped me make it better and cleaner (in alphabetic order):
Abdulrahman Alhadhrami, Olga Arnoldi, Ruslan Dibirov, Yurii Dubinka, Sergey Dudal, Artem Dunaev, Karin Eriksson, Carl Frenn, Maksym Ivanov, Oleksandr Kovalchuk, Artem Koshkov, Julia Kuznetsova, Dmitry Levonevskiy, Vincent van der Linden, Enrique Pablo Molinari, Miroslav Olenskij, Mikhail Popov, Nikita Puzankov, Satrio Adi Rukmono, Alexey Rykhalskiy, Anatoly Severin, Pavel Stepanets, Maksim Yakunin, Zhen Yao, Grigory Zaripov.

Want to see your name in this list in the next edition? Just send your thoughts to `book@yegor256.com`. I reply to all emails.

And, of course, thanks to Andreea Mironiuc for the cactus with a nipple on the cover.

Preface

They say that there are four principles in Object-Oriented Programming (OOP), which are encapsulation, abstraction, inheritance, and polymorphism. Honestly, I have a very vague understanding of what ~~these words mean~~ they mean by these words. Every time I hear them I feel scared that someone may ask me whether I know the meaning. Will I teach them to you? I will try not to. I believe they were invented by some "industry experts" and "scientists," who have never wrote a single working piece of software in their lives.

This book is not for you, if you want to be one of them. This book is for you, if you want to become a programmer, who writes software: 1) that works, 2) well paid, and 3) is fun to write. Those four fancy words will only take the fun away from you. This book is not a formal explanation of object-oriented programming and most probably will not help you pass a single job interview. But it will help you fall in love with the process of writing code. Just like I did, many years ago.

In the next two hundred pages, under my supervision, you will create a web game, which you will be able to demonstrate to your friends and they will play it. You will start from the ground level, assumingly having absolutely no knowledge in programming. You will finish as a programmer who is passionate enough to create a new Google.

Chapter 1

First

I decided to write this book in response to multiple requests from junior programmers: they asked me to explain OOP in simple words. However, when I started writing it, I realized that to have these simple words, I had to introduce them first, and make sure we understood them right. That's how the content you will read now was born. The first chapter is not about object-oriented programming at all, it's not even about programming specifically. It is about computers. We have to understand how they work before we start writing code for them.

Each section ends with a few exercises. The stars in front of each question, depict the difficulty level. Unlike textbook problem sets, which tend to rehash material you already covered, these are to help you learn more than what's in the section. They force you to step off the guided path and explore on your own. They will make you research other languages, figure out how to implement features, or otherwise get you to strike out on your own. Vanquish them, and you'll come away with a broader understanding and possibly a few bumps and scrapes. Or skip them if you want to stay inside the comfy confines of the tour bus. It's your book.

Let me quote you one of the reviewers, who made a great summary of the book structure: "It's like this book tries to explain how to build the empire state building, so you start (Chapter 1 and 2) with explaining what a house is, what a human being is, a little bit of anthropology, what a nail is, what a hammer is, what wood is, and then you tell the reader to learn about all other tools and cement himself by outside reading. Then (Chapter 3) you talk about how societies moved from simple farming with simple houses to big cities and big buildings, and you talk about supply chains of manufacturing and architecture equipment. Then in Chapter 4 you start building the first room in the building, and towards the end of the chapter, you build 99% of the building." It seems to be pretty accurate.

1.1 Hardware

Did you already get yourself a computer? A laptop. A MacBook™. I know that it's expensive, but do you want to love what you are doing? Do you want to enjoy writing code? Do you want to be rich and famous? You have to start with a proper tool. You will have to deal with a lot of stress while programming and a lot of frustration. You will only do yourself a very bad favor if your computer will run on Windows™.

Windows is not suitable for programmers. If you meet anyone

who will tell you otherwise, you must know that you deal with a bad programmer, or a poor one, which are the same things. Your computer has to be MacBook (I have to admit sadly that the last stable version was made in 2015). Otherwise, you won't become a great programmer. Get a used one if you don't have money for a new one, but don't even think about buying one of those ASUS™, Dell™, or Lenovo™ pieces of garbage. They are not bad by themselves, it's the Windows they install is what makes them garbage.

Let's discuss the difference between so-called *hardware* and *software*. Hardware is what you hold in your hands when you buy it: a box with a keyboard, a screen, and a power adapter. This is called hardware. It's made of steel, plastic, and silicon (that's why Silicon Valley, by the way). Your laptop is pretty lightweight now, but many years ago, computers were pretty heavy and really *hard*. That's why they got this name: hard-ware. So, anything that you can touch—your laptop, your mobile phone, your electronic watch, your fridge, and even your bicycle—is called hardware nowadays.

Software is what makes these pieces of steel, plastic, and silicon look like a thinking machine. Software is the *commands* your hardware *executes*. When you turn your MacBook on, it shows a logo of Apple™ at the center of the screen (it did for me this morning). When the laptop is turned off, its battery is not connected to the screen, and the screen is dark. When you turn it on, the electricity from the battery goes to the big piece of silicon inside the laptop, also known as the Central Processor Unit (CPU), and to the screen. The screen turns on and is still dark because nobody told it what to show you. The CPU, when the electricity is inside it, has to decide what pixels on the screen should be white, and which of them should remain dark.

The decision is pretty complex, as you can imagine. The Apple logo is a pretty complex piece of art and includes thousands of pixels. By the way, do you realize that your screen is just a large matrix of pixels? In my MacBook, there are 2880x1800 pixels on my display. The width of the display is 2880, and the height is 1800. You can imagine how small are those pixels! Each pixel can be black, white, or one of the other 16 million colors. That's right, sixteen million! Thus, there are 5.2 million pixels in my MacBook's display, and they all are black when the laptop is turned off. When I turn it on, the electricity gets into all of these pixels, but they still don't know what colors out of that 16-million palette to choose. Pixels, as you already understand, are the hardware.

Now the CPU has to decide which pixels to turn white to show the Apple logo. I don't know the exact count, but there will be thousands of them in the logo. The CPU has to give thousands of *commands* to the screen in order to *render* the logo. They may look like this:

```
PAINT 33, 7, white
PAINT 34, 7, white
PAINT 35, 7, white
```

There are three commands to tell the screen to make three pixels white at the positions `(33,7)`, `(34,7)`, and `(35,7)`. If the first number is the x coordinate and the second number is the y coordinate, you can imagine what will be the figure these three commands will draw.

★
Find a piece of paper, a pen, and write a program using the command `PAINT`, which will draw a `:)` smile. Make those "eyes" blue and the lips red.

★
Explain what exactly silicon is doing inside your laptop.

★
Explain what GPU is for.

★
Explain the difference between RGB and CMYK.

★
Name three other very popular screen resolutions, which first versions of Apple computers had had.

★★
Why pixels are black, instead of being white, when electricity is not going through?

★★
I said above that each pixel can be of one of those Sixteen million different colors, but the exact number of colors is not 16,000,000. What is the exact number and why?

★★
Explain the difference between RAM and ROM.

★★
Explain how Z1, Mark I, and ENIAC computers were different from each other.

★★★
Explain the architecture of x86 CPU.

1.2 Software

This was our first piece of *software*. It is written by programmers and then *deployed* to the CPU so that the CPU can *execute* it. Without software, the CPU can't do anything, because it won't know where to put the pixels. It knows how to talk to the screen, it knows how to deliver commands to the screen, but it doesn't have the commands. A programmer has to write these commands, just like we just did.

Usually, people who create hardware are not the same people who write software. The CPU in my MacBook was manufactured by Intel™ Corp., a silicon chips maker from California, the screen in my MacBook was made by LG™ Display Inc., a company from South Korea, and assembled by Apple factory in China.

The software that draws that nice Apple logo on the screen when I turn on my MacBook was made by Apple and is called an *Operating System* (OS), I don't know exactly why. Maybe because it helps us "operate" our hardware and other pieces of software. OS is the first software that starts when the computer is turned on. As you can imagine, there could be many different operating systems for the same piece of hardware. Apple Inc. gives its customers the operating system known as macOS™.

Microsoft Inc., a software company from Redmond, creates its operating system, which is called Windows. When you buy a Lenovo laptop, it already has Windows *installed*. When you buy a MacBook, it has macOS installed. But you can replace it, of course. You can install Windows on your MacBook. It will work. It won't work great, but it will work. Why not great? Because a software is often created for a specific hardware and if the hardware is not as expected, the software gets confused. For example, if you install macOS on Lenovo, it will attempt to find a screen with exactly 2880x1800 pixels. Obviously, the screen in the Lenovo laptop has a different number of pixels, and the software won't understand how to draw the Apple logo right.

That's why operating systems are either created specifically for the hardware they are supposed to work with (like macOS for MacBook) or they don't work well (like Windows for Lenovo). Windows is supposed to work well with Lenovo, ASUS, and many other types of computers, while macOS is made to work only with the hardware manufactured by Apple Inc. It seems that the one-for-all strategy is suitable for a mass market, where Microsoft is dominating, while Apple's exclusivity is for the high-end market, where they are the only and the primary player at the moment. This is, by the way, why I'm recommending you get a MacBook.

You can write your OS for your MacBook, which will work even better than macOS. Of course, it will draw your avatar instead of the Apple logo when your MacBook starts. But it will take a lot of time to create such a big piece of software. Operating systems are usually considered to be the largest software products created by programmers. They usually are created by big companies with a lot of programmers and money, but not always. There are operating systems created by software enthusiasts, and they, just like Windows, work with any possible hardware. Linux™ and FreeBSD™ are the most popular among others. And I don't recommend them to you (for learning programming), for the same reason: they work with everything, but don't work well with anything. So, MacBook with macOS is your best choice.

★
Do you know what parts your laptop is made of and who their manufacturers are? Who made the screen, the keyboard, the CPU, the motherboard, who wrote the software and who assembled pieces together?

★
Do you know what OEM software is?

★★
I was wrong above when I said that the OS is the software that starts right after the computer is turned on. It is not. What is the name of the software the starts before the OS?

★★
Tell the history of macOS, starting from PDP-7.

★★
Name ten other operating systems and explain who they were made by and what for.

★★★
Read *The UNIX Programming Environment (1984)* by Kernighan, Pike, et al. [12].

1.3 File

Now, let's quickly create our first program and call it a day. You will need to turn on the laptop and start a Terminal. Do you know how to do it? Figure it out yourself, should be easy. When it starts you will see a new *window* with a ~~black~~ white background. The top line of the window will show a blinking *cursor*. This line is called a *command line*. You will post commands there and the operating system will understand and *execute* them. Try to type `echo Hello` and see what happens.

This command line is your interface to the operating system. That's how you communicate with it, if you are a programmer (I strongly advice you to stay far away from graphic user interfaces and stick to the command line). You create files, move them around, copy, delete, edit, compile, and execute. Wait, do you know what a file is? What about directory? I'm sure you do, but let me go over it again, just to be clear we are on the same page.

There is a so called *file system* that helps us organize our software. Do you know how how many commands (CPU instructions) are in macOS software? I don't know the exact number, but definitely more than fifty millions. If we put them all in one list, it will be impossible to read it. It will be too long. We have to break this large volume of commands and data into smaller pieces. That's why they invented files and directories, many years ago. There is a *root directory* in your MacBook. You can see what's there just by saying `ls /` to the command line.

The root directory is the starting point of your file system. It has files and sub-directories. Each sub-directory has files and sub-directories, and so on. Programmers usually present the directory structure like this:

```
/
  usr/
    local/
      bin/
    var/
    lib/
  etc/
    aliases
```

Here `usr` and `etc` are the directories at the first level. They are sub-directories of the root directory. The `local` directory is inside `usr` and is on the second level after the root. The full *path* of the `bin` directory is `/usr/local/bin`.

In the file system tree above `/etc/aliases` is a file. A directory is like an office folder that contains other folders or files, while a file may only contain some *content* and may not include any other files or directories inside. A file path can be pretty long, for example this one (the backslash here is not a typo):

`/Library/Image\ Capture/Support/Icons/my-icon.jpg`

The directory you are currently in is called *current directory*. In order to find out what is your current directory, say `pwd` to the command line. You should get the path of your current directory. To see the list of files and directories in your current directory just say `ls`.

One more thing before we start writing code. You also have a so called *home directory*, where all your work is supposed to be stored. You don't want to keep your work files in the root directory. That directory is only for the files that only the operating system knows what to do with. Your files, like the program we will write now, should be kept in your home directory. This is how you go into it: `cd ~`. Do it now and then print your current directory again: `pwd`. In my case it is `/Users/yegor`. Yours is similar, I believe.

Let's create a new directory: `mkdir jo`. Here `mkdir` is a command we are giving to the operating system (stands for "make directory") and `jo` is a name of a new directory I just made up (stands for "junior objects"). The directory should be created. Say `ls` to see whether it is there. You should see it in the list, among other files and directories you already have in

your home directory. Now, let's go into this new directory:
`cd jo`. Here `cd` is a command to the operating system (stands for "change directory") and `jo` is the name of the directory we just created. Now, let's see what is inside this directory: `ls`. It should be empty. There will be no names printed out.

Now, let's create a new file in this directory: `touch a.html`. Here, `touch` is a command that means "create a new file if it doesn't exist" and `a.html` is the name of the file. The file should be created. Let's check by saying `ls`. The file is empty, but it is there. By empty I mean that there is no content inside. We just created it but it doesn't have anything inside. It's a perfectly legal situation, sometimes files don't have any content and their *length* is zero.

Now, let's open this file in Safari. Just say `open -a Safari a.html`. You should see a new window opened and it has to be just white blank. Get back to the Terminal window now and get ready to write some code.

Here is how you do it:

```
echo "Hello, <b>world</b>" > a.html
```

Here `echo` is the command which takes what is in the quotes and prints to where we say it to print it. We say, by using `> a.html`, that the text has to be printed into the file `a.html`. The text inside the quotes is this:

```
Hello, <b>world</b>
```

This is our first program. Go back to Safari and reload the page (click ⌘+R). What do you see? I see "Hello, **world**." Safari somehow magically understood that by `<b>` and `</b>` we meant "Make the 'world' bold!"

———

★
Why do you think I crossed the word "black" in the first paragraph of this section and wrote "white" instead?

★
Why the blinking rectangle in the Terminal is called a cursor?

★
What does `cd -` do?

★★
The `touch` command is not actually doing what I said above. What is it doing exactly?

★★
Explain the difference between SDD and HDD.

★★
What a backslash `\` doing in the file path above? Write this file path without using the backslash.

★★
Find a way to see what is inside the file (the content) using Terminal commands, without Safari.

★★
Say `ls -al` while being in an empty directory. Explain what those `.` and `..` things are for.

★★
Study Unix pipelines and make a one-line command, which will find count how many lines in a text file contain a specific piece of text (use `cat`, `grep`, and `wc`).

★★★
Find the longest file path in the file system of your laptop.

★ ★ ★

Learn the most popular 30 bash commands.

★ ★ ★

Learn *touch typing* and make sure your speed is 50+ WPM.

1.4 Program

As you already understand, a program is a text that both a computer and a programmer can understand. A program can be long, like that multi-million *lines of code* operating system written by coders from Apple; or pretty short, just like this one-line program we just created. A line of code (LoC) is a line of text. There are also kilo lines of code (KLoC) and mega lines of code (MLoC). Do you know what kilo and mega stand for? It's for thousands and millions, right? Wrong. Well, it's right for lines of code, but wrong for kilobytes and megabytes. I'm sure you've heard about them, but let me explain one more time so that you never fail a job interview—this is where they like to ask questions about *binary* numbers so often.

Binary numbers are just a way computers represent numbers. Let's say you are 17 years old. There are two digits in this number: `1` and `7`. They stay together and the `1` goes before `7`. Why is that? Because `1` has to be multiplied by `10` and then `7` has to be added. This is called a *decimal* number, because we multiply by ten. With the number `1976`, we multiply `7` by ten, `9` by a hundred and `1` by a thousand in order to know the actual value of the number.

Binary numbers are exactly the same, but the multiplier is two, not ten. For example, the number `11` in binary means three, because we multiply the left `1` by two, not by ten. The next position will be multiplied by four, the next one by eight, and then by 16 and so on.

I would suggest you pause with this book and read about binary numbers somewhere in the Internet. You don't need to understand them in order to continue reading this book, but I strongly recommend studying this subject. If you are a mathematician deep inside, you will enjoy it. If you are not, you may want to ask yourself a question regarding whether you really need to become a programmer.

I will wait here until you investigate this subject properly.

OK, you're back. Now you're ready to answer the question asked above. How many bytes a does a kilobyte contain? Not a thousand. There are 1,024. How many in are a megabyte? Not a million. There are 1,048,576 bytes. Why? You tell me.

★
After finishing writing this book, I was advised by one of the reviewers that a kilobyte, according to the decision made by the International Electrotechnical Commission (IEC) in 1998, contains 1,000 (10^3) bytes, while a data unit of 1,024 (2^{10}) bytes has a different name. Which one is it?

★
Write your year of birth as a binary number.

★
How many bits an does an unsigned four-bytes integer contain?

★
How many bits are in 16 petabytes?

★ ★
Sort this list of numbers written in C language: 0x6F, 0154, 107, and 0b1101100.

★ ★
Write a negative binary number and explain how arithmetic operations (addition and subtraction) work with it. Convert +234 and -180 to binary numbers and calculate their sum.

★ ★
Name three different *signed number representations* and explain how they work.

★ ★ ★
Explain how numbers with a floating point are stored by computers.

1.5 Language

The program we just created is written in HTML. It's a *programming language*. Computers, unlike us, understand many languages. A lot of languages. There are thousands of programming languages that exist in the world and some of them are very popular, others less so. One day you will create your own language and will teach your laptop to understand it. Until that day comes, you have to learn the languages invented by other programmers. For example, the HTML language was invented by Tim Berners-Lee in 1991. It's pretty simple and you already know one command of HTML: `<b>...</b>`. This command makes the text within the *markup elements* look bold.

When HTML language was created there were only 18 elements

in it. This `<b>` was one of them. It was—and still is—a pretty simple language. You can learn it in a few hours. Other languages like Java, C++, JavaScript, Ruby, SQL, Python, or C# are much more complex and may require several months or years to learn them well. To become a professional programmer, you will have to choose a few languages to study and dive deeper into them. In this book we will use two languages: HTML and JavaScript. Why two? Because they are both required to create the software we are going to create: a web application. This happens very often when a few languages are needed for one software *module*.

Don't be scared, you don't need to know them all. You don't even need to know those few languages you choose well. I don't think I know everything about Java, even though I've been using it for over 15 years. There are still some blank spots for me but I don't think I need to learn them. I can use Java without knowing everything in it, just like English. I can speak it knowing just a few thousand words of it and it's not my mother tongue. Of course, I constantly try to improve my English and Java skills, but I don't worry when I realize that there is still a lot to learn.

Take a look at HTML. As I mentioned, there were 18 elements when it was invented. I was using it in 1993 and I didn't know all of them. Do you know how many are out there at the time of writing? 108. And they keep adding new elements every year. Do I know them all? Not really. Do I need to know them all? If I was a professional HTML designer, most likely, yes. But I'm not; I'm a Java programmer.

Programming languages are not set in stone. They are born and they die. They get new commands and they get rid of unnecessary commands. Just like what happens with the English language. A few years ago I was at a job interview as a candidate, and they told me that English was losing many words every century. Their question was: how many? They wanted me to calculate it. I remember that the numbers I got were in thousands.

You may wonder, how does the computer understand what language we are currently speaking with it? It looks at the file *extension*. The file we created is called `a.html`. Here, `a` is the name and `html` is the extension. It was invented specifically to give the computer a hint as to what language is inside the file. A file with a JavaScript program inside would be named as `prog1.js`, for example. You can use any extension, but neither the computer nor other programmers will understand if you name your HTML file as `t.x`. The extension `x` is not attributed to any programming language (to my knowledge).

★
Name ten of the most popular programming languages, and explain what they were created for and what advantages they have compared to others.

★
Name twenty of the most popular file extensions and explain what types of content they are attributed to.

★ ★
Strictly speaking, HTML is not a programming language, but a *markup* language because it's not *Turing complete*. Explain what this means.

★ ★
Name two HTML elements that were *deprecated* and explain why this has happened.

29

★ ★ ★

Calculate how many English words were lost in the 19th century.

★ ★ ★

Name 16 of the most notable programming languages created since 1948, starting from Plankalkül, and describe their unique features.

★ ★ ★

Read *XML in a Nutshell (2004)* by Harold, Means, and Udemadu [10].

1.6 IDE

Let's try to write a bigger HTML program in `a.html` and see how Safari will understand it. Let's put this code into it:

```
<p style="font-size:20px">
  My ideas are
  <span style="font-size:4em">Big</span>
  but my budget is
  <span style="font-size:0.5em">Small</span>
</p>
```

Just put it into the `a.html` file and reload the page in Safari. Wait, you don't know how to do it? You will need a *text editor* for that. It's another application you need to have on your computer in order to work with the *source code*. Let's try TextEdit, which is on your MacBook. Write this in the command line:

```
open -a TextEdit a.html
```

A new window will pop up and you will see the text we have

there now. You can edit it and then save. When you're done, reload the web page in Safari and tell me what you see. Do you understand the HTML program? There are two new elements for you: `<p>` and `<span>`. There are also `style` attributes. I won't explain how they work, you can see it visually.

The bigger question now is whether you will stay with the primitive TextEdit editor or get something better for yourself. Professional programmers, including myself, work in what are called IDEs (Integrated Development Environments). You may also want to get one. They are basically text editors with many additional features, which make your life easier. Good IDEs are not free (you'd spend $130 for a full-featured version of WebStorm™ from JetBrains™, for example), but they are worth the money you spend.

In this book we will stay with TextEdit, which is free, but keep in mind that as soon as you get a bit more interested in programming, you should get WebStorm (or something similar) and work like a pro.

★
Name three other popular IDEs, install their trial versions, and decide which one you like the best.

★
Actually, some IDEs are good and free at the same time. Name three of them, install them, and pick the one you like the best.

★★
Learn how `vim` text editor works and create an HTML document in it.

★ ★

Write an HTML program that will render a spreadsheet of your monthly budget. The columns should be labeled as "Date," "Title," and "Amount." Make sure your font size is 22px and pick the right font from Google Fonts.

★ ★

Read *Dynamic HTML (2002)* by Goodman [9].

1.7 Runtime

When you are editing an `.html` file, the computer doesn't care what's going on. The computer doesn't watch you modifying it nor does it try to understand your program in the file. It's just a text file for the computer, which may contain a program or a letter to your roommate.

The computer starts *interpreting* your text and understanding the commands you put there only when you ask it to do so. When you ask Safari to open the page with your HTML program inside, Safari starts looking into the `a.html` file, reading it line by line, and attempting to translate each command into pixels on your screen. In the end, the text you see on the screen of your laptop is just a collection of many small pixels. Some of them are black, others are white.

Say you tell Safari this:

```
Hello, <b>World</b>
```

You don't say anything about any pixels. Safari reads your `<p>` command and decides that more black pixels are needed at this particular area of the screen because you want the word `World` to look bolder. You talk to Safari in HTML language, and Safari talks to the CPU in another language that is much less beautiful than HTML. It's called Assembly, and you don't want to learn it. Here is what our "Hello, world" program looks in Assembly:

```
push    ds
xor     ax, ax
push    ax
mov     ax, data
mov     ds, ax
mov     es, ax
mov     ah, 30h
int     21h
cmp     al, 2
jae     dev1
mov     dx, offset msg2
jmp     dev6
```

I have no idea what I just wrote, to be honest. I just found a small piece of Assembly code on the Internet and copied it here. My point is—and I'm sure you get it—that it's cryptic and no sane person would want to write programs in Assembly. Except for those smart folks who created Safari. We should be very thankful to them. Many years ago, when I was a school kid, there was no Safari on the market and we had to write our programs or parts of them in Assembly very often. That was thirty years ago.

Since then, many software *interpreters* like Safari have been created. They take your code written in a simple and good-looking language like HTML, *run* it, and convert it into Assembly commands known as *instructions*. The time when this happens is called *run time* (or just *runtime*), and Safari and similar products are called *runtime environments*. While your code is in a text file, it's in its *development time*. When Safari starts reading it and translating into Assembly, it's in its runtime.

There is also *testing time*, which we will discuss later, and *compile time*, which exists for some programming languages, but not for HTML and JavaScript, which we will use in this book.

Every time you hit ⌘+R in Safari, runtime starts. It takes microseconds to finish since modern computers are really fast. However, you have to remember that Safari does a lot of work behind the scenes understanding your HTML commands and translating them into Assembly instructions, which are then understood by the CPU, which makes those small pixels black or white.

There are tens of thousands of Assembly instructions to be executed for a single `<b>` in your HTML program. Maybe even hundreds of thousands. Do you know what that GHz parameter of your laptop stands for? The specification of my MacBook says that its CPU runs at a speed of 2.3GHz. This means that every second it executes 2,300,000,000 instructions. Thus, if page reloading takes, say, two seconds, this means that the program Safari interprets gets translated into about 5 billion Assembly instructions. Five billion! We don't want to write five billion lines of code just to say "Hello, World." We want *higher-level* languages.

★
Name five languages that need compile time.

★
How many instructions can the fastest computer execute per second?

★ ★
Write a program in Assembly to swap values between `AX` and `BX` registers.

★ ★
Explain the difference between RISC and CISC computers.

★ ★
Explain how virtual machines works: GraalVM and LLVM.

★ ★
I was wrong when I said that 2.3GHz meant that the CPU executes 2.3 billion instructions per second. What exactly does this number mean?

★ ★
I was not exactly correct in saying that two seconds between hitting ⌘+R and seeing a fully rendered page are spent on executing five billion instructions. What else is happening during this time?

★ ★ ★
Write an HTML program that will be interpreted differently by Safari and Firefox, and the pages they render will have visual differences.

★ ★ ★
Name four of the most popular CPU instruction sets and explain the differences between them.

1.8 Abstraction

Assembly is a low-level programming language, while HTML is a high-level language. The difference is not only in the number of lines of code, but mostly in the amount of details that are visible to the programmer. When you write a program in Assembly, you can do so many things with the CPU, screen, pixels, memory, and anything else you can only imagine. All pieces of the hardware in the laptop are standing right in front of you, waiting for instructions.

This is not the case in HTML. With HTML, you can only do a few things and that's it. You can say "Hello, World" or "Good-bye, mom." Nothing else. Well, I'm kidding, the variety of options is way larger than that, but still much smaller than what Assembly lets you do with, for example, the screen.

Here is a simple example. No matter what do you in your HTML *document*, no matter how complex is your HTML code, you can't draw anything outside of the page. Everything you *render*, will stay within the borders of the Safari window. This is your territory of freedom and you can't get out of it. With Assembly, you can make any pixel on the screen black, no matter where it is located, inside the Safari window or anywhere else.

Thus, Assembly is more powerful? Definitely. It is the most powerful and complex instrument for programmers. Is HTML less powerful? Of course. HTML is super primitive, but is it less powerful? I can write just one line of code that would take millions of lines in Assembly. I spend just a few minutes doing what Assembly programmers would spend months on. So, who's got the power?

These are different powers and levels of *abstraction*. Assembly is a language with a very low level of abstraction. It deals with small details and gives a lot of power for those who care about these details. HTML is a language of much higher abstraction. It is powerful for those who want to get things done faster and don't want to worry about less important details.

It seems that the world is moving towards languages of higher abstraction. Where would we be without them? We wouldn't have so much software around us if we still wrote programs in Assembly like we were doing when I was a kid. Programs written in more abstract languages are easier to read and understand. Let me show a practical example within the language you already know. This is HTML5 (the fifth version of HTML *released* in 2014, 23 years after the release of the first version):

```
<video width="1920px" height="1080px">
  <source src="birthday.mp4" type="video/mp4">
</video>
```

This code, as you most probably understand, will tell Safari to show a video player with the `birthday.mp4` file inside. The size of the video player will be 1920x1080 pixels, and the format of the video file is MP4. Do you know how many lines of code the first version of HTML required a programmer to write to achieve the same results? Try to find out and you will be impressed. It was a complex task that required a lot of time and brainpower. Now it's just three simple lines of code. HTML designers did us a very good favor; they lifted us to to a higher level of abstraction. Of course, we lost something because of that. The code we had to write before gave us much more control over the video displayed. We had an option to render different buttons there; it was possible to make it look the way we want; and so on. Now, all video players look identical on the Internet because programmers are using HTML5 and let Safari decide the details.

The abstraction principle is applicable not only to programming languages, but to everything else you will meet later in this book. Higher levels of abstraction make things more, well, "abstract," which means ease of use and simplicity. This is what we programmers need in most cases. Sometimes—very rarely—we may need to get into the details and deal with something more specific, like that video player. But this must only be an exception and you should try to hide the details and make them invisible as much as possible.

★ ★

Name five more abstract features of HTML5 that didn't exist earlier.

★ ★ ★

Create an HTML page that will play your MP4 video file without using the `<video>` element of HTML5.

1.9 Maintainability

For the vast majority of tasks we programmers have to solve, the higher the level of abstraction the better. It's better for us and other programmers. The fewer lines of code we write and the fewer details we deal with, the easier it will be for them, our fellow coders, to *understand* and to *maintain* the code. It's extremely important these days. We programmers have to think about the quality of our code to make it *maintainable*.

Time is what matters now. Not the time of reloading the page in Safari, as some of you might think. This is not as important anymore since computers are pretty fast, as we found out just a few pages ago. They execute billions of instructions every second and will do even more when this book is published. I can't even imagine how fast they will be in ten years; very fast. But we programmers will be "slower" and more expensive since our working time will cost more than it does now. Maybe that's why you decided to become a programmer, isn't it?

Companies will care how much they pay programmers and how much they lose when a programmer writes a program, quits the project, and nobody can understand what has been written there. The program would have to be rewritten and a new budget would need to be spent. It was not as critical thirty years ago since our salaries were much lower and computers were much slower. Instead, it was very important how fast the code was. Not anymore. What matters now is how *readable* your code is.

The faster I can understand your code, the better it is. For example, this is very readable code:

```
Hello, <b>World</b>
```

This one, however, is much less readable, even though it does the exact same thing and renders the exact same page in Safari:

```
<span
style="
  font-size:1em"    >Hello,
<B>Wo<span>rld</    span></b></SPAN>
```

The page will look the same in Safari, but is it something your fellow programmer will enjoy reading? This code has a lot of *redundancy* and it's badly formatted. The maintainability of this code is very low and it's a sin many programmers have to confess to committing. You don't want to be a sinner of that kind. Your code has to be easy to read and look pretty.

Your value as a programmer for the project you will work for will be much higher if you write maintainable and easy to understand code. You will make more money, to put it simply. Later in the book, we will return to this problem many times. I will reiterate that the way our code looks matters a lot. It has to be pretty; just making it work is not enough. We are not hackers from the '80s, anymore. The era of elegant code is coming.

I think you are asking yourself now: How do I make my code look pretty? What are the recipes? Even though we haven't written many lines of code yet, this is the right time to discuss it. There are indeed a few recipes.

First, make it simple. If you look at it and think that it's complex, you're most likely doing something wrong. You, the author, should be confident that your code is simple—very simple—and you can't make it any simpler. If you can, do so. Smart programmers don't write complex code. No matter how complex the problem is, the code should look simple. Later in the book, we will write pretty complex pieces of software and you may find it pretty difficult to understand sometimes. Don't blame yourself. Blame the author of the code, which is me. Always. It's not your fault if you can't understand something in the code; it's the failure of its author. What do you think about this line of code:

`Hello, <b>World</b>`

Do you have any problems understanding it? Did I explain what those `<b>` and `</b>` meant to you beforehand? I didn't. Did I explain the difference between them and the meaning of the slash symbol in front of the second `<b>` to you? I didn't. Did you get it yourself? I'm sure you did. The first `<b>` opens the part of the text that is supposed to be bold and the second `</b>` closes it. You probably understand what `<i>World</i>` would mean now, right? If I tell you that `b` stands for "bold," what do you think `i` stands for?

★

Why did you decide to become a programmer? Name three main reasons.

★ ★

Find three metrics that measure source code quality or maintainability.

★ ★

Name four famous coding conventions/standards. Pick the one you like the most and explain your choice.

★ ★

Make the "Hello, World" example even more unmaintainable and difficult to read than the sample I suggested.

1.10 Documentation

Good code should explain itself, even for a reader who has almost no idea what the code is about, how it works, or who it was written for. Some programmers still believe that good code has to have *documentation*. Indeed, years ago, when programming languages were at a very low level of abstraction, like Assembly, they needed documentation. Otherwise, it was very difficult or almost impossible to understand what it meant. Check this out (I found it on the Internet and I have no idea what it does):

```
        LXI H 2000H
        MOV A, M
        MVI C, 08H
        MVI B, 00H
    j2: RAL
        JNC j1
        INR B
    j1: DCR C
        JNZ j2
        HLT
```

Do you understand what is going on here? I don't. Nobody does. How about the same piece of Assembly code, but with supporting *inline* documentation:

```
        LXI H 2000H  ;HL points at location 2000H
        MOV A, M     ;Loads A with the content of M
        MVI C, 08H   ;Sets up counter for number of bits
        MVI B, 00H   ;Sets counter to count number of ones
    j2: RAL          ;Rotates accmltr left through carry
        JNC j1       ;On no carry jumps to j1:
        INR B        ;Increases counter B by one
    j1: DCR C        ;Decreases counter C by one
        JNZ j2       ;When C is not zero jumps to j2:
        HLT          ;Terminates the program
```

It's still cryptic and difficult to understand since we both are not Assembly programmers (I was, but many years ago). However, the *comments* by the end of each line do us a favor. The computer doesn't read them; they are ignored. In Assembly, anything that goes after the ; (semi-colon) at the end of the line is ignored. These comments are called *inline* since they stay on the same line with the code they support. In Assembly, their presence was crucial. However, in modern programming languages of a much higher level of abstraction, they have the opposite effect.

How about we add an inline comment to our HTML code (comments in HTML start with `<!--` and end with `-->`):

```
Hello, <b>World</b> <!-- Make "World" look bolder -->
```

Does it help to have this comment here? Isn't it obvious what this line of code is without the silly comment? It is. The comment here is definitely *redundant*. However, how about the bad code we've seen before:

```
<span
style="
   font-size:1em"    >Hello,
<B>Wo<span>rld</    span></b></SPAN>
```

This "beauty" definitely needs comments. I can't understand why its author, for example, says `font-size:1em` since this HTML attribute won't have any effect. It basically says that the size of the font should remain the same as it was before. The default font size is `1em` and the code instructs Safari to set it to `1em` once again. Why? I don't know and I need an explanation. I need a comment, badly. Something like this:

```
<span
style="
   <!-- We are setting to 1em here because ... -->
   font-size:1em"    >Hello,
<B>Wo<span>rld</    span></b></SPAN>
```

Now this comment helps. Well, a bit. The code is still messy, badly formatted, and very difficult to read and understand. There should be many inline comments to allow us readers understand the intent of the code author. Why is the *opening* tag `<span>` in *lower case* (all letters are small), while the *closing* tag

`</SPAN>` is in *upper case* (all letters are capital)? At the same time, the opening tag `<B>` is in upper case and the closing `</b>` is in lower case. It's a mystery. Moreover, in one place `</ span>` has spaces between the slash and the `span`, while in all other cases there are no spaces. There is a severe lack of *consistency* in design and coding decisions the author of the code made.

When I was a kid of about 12 years old, I remember seeing my first book about programming. It was about Basic, one of the first high-level languages, which was supposed to be simpler than Assembly and help junior programmers get up to speed fast. I was really junior, both young and without almost any experience in programming. There was an example of a Basic program in that book (it wasn't really a book; it was actually a very short 40-page manual) that I had to type in and execute. Most of the lines were more or less easy to understand, but I remember one line that puzzled me a lot. Here is how that program looked:

```
10 PRINT "Enter a number:"
20 INPUT X
30 FOR I=1 TO 9
40 PRINT X,"*",I,"=",(X*I)
50 NEXT I
```

Even if you know Basic, pretend that you don't and you're twelve years old. Do you understand this piece of code? I remember that I had no problems with the first three lines, however line `40` was big trouble for me. It looked like a combination of symbols with absolutely no meaning. What made it worse is that the person who gave me the book didn't know either and had been telling me that programmers sometimes don't need to understand what those symbols meant, but had to just type them the way the documentation said. I refused the idea of me becoming a "symbols typist." I wanted to know what they meant and the

code itself was not giving many hints. Look at it again:
`X,"*",I,"=",(X*I)`. What?

Of course, there were no inline comments around. Just this random collection of symbols that even I've had problems finding on the keyboard. If I wrote that book about Basic now, I would add some comments (in Basic, comments start with `REM` and the rest of the line is ignored):

```
10 PRINT "Enter a number:"
20 INPUT X
30 FOR I=1 TO 9
31 REM Here we will print the line, which
32 REM consists of five parts, concatenated with
33 REM the comma:
40 PRINT X,"*",I,"=",(X*I)
50 NEXT I
```

Better now? I guess. But how about this code instead:

```
10 PRINT "Enter a number:"
20 INPUT X
30 FOR I=1 TO 9
40 PRINT X
41 PRINT "*"
42 PRINT I
43 PRINT "="
44 PRINT X * I
50 NEXT I
```

Now it's obvious, isn't it? Especially for someone who sees Basic for the first time and is expected to fall in love with programming. This code is longer and much more readable. It is less cryptic and explains itself.

My point is that only badly written code needs inline comments. If the code is clean and elegant by itself, it doesn't need comments attached to its lines. When someone tells you that your code needs documentation because it is difficult to understand, don't rush writing documentation. Also, when you read someone's code and have a hard time understanding it, don't blame yourself for being not smart enough. It's not your fault. The code that you read should be easy to digest. Otherwise, it's bad code. The code that we will start writing in a few pages will not be perfect. Don't blame yourself for not being able to understand some parts of it. It's not your fault, it's my fault. My job as an author of the code is to make it work not only on your computer, but also easy to process by your brain. Your brains are the most important consumer of my code.

To be honest, not all programmers you will meet will agree with this philosophy. Most of them, especially some experienced ones, will believe that the more complex the code they write, the better programmers they are. They will think that they are superior to you because they understand something that you don't. They are wrong. Senior programmers don't write code that junior programmers can't understand. Instead, senior programmers write code that is so easy to understand that you, a junior programmer, can find it interesting to read and even modify. Don't be scared of them, senior and proud of themselves. They're not professional if they write something similar to the first Basic example above.

There is another type of documentation a source code may have, which is called *block comments*. They may look like this, in case of our simple HTML program:

```
<!--
This pages introduces the system to its
users and welcomes them.  The page was
created by Yegor Bugayenko,  an  author
this book.  If you have any ideas about
this page, email me at me@yegor256.com.
-->
Hello, <b>World</b>
```

This type of comment is always helpful. It explains what the reader should expect to see in the file. What it was created for, who wrote it, where to send an email if something doesn't work as expected, and so on. This information is helpful and it adds value to the program. You should always start writing a program with this comment on top of the file. Also, it's *best practice* to have a block comment in front of every block of code, like a function, method, or module.

★

Name five of some other best practices of programming.

★ ★

Compare 10 large Java projects from GitHub[TM] and find out how much license documentation text they have in front of every source file.

★ ★

Study three JavaScript projects in GitHub and find places where inline comments are redundant.

Chapter 2

Second

It's time to start writing some object-oriented code in JavaScript. We won't write anything serious in this chapter, but will instead study the most important concepts of OOP: object, encapsulation, type, scope of visibility, variable, operator, attribute, method, statement, constructor, and so on. You may wonder why JavaScript was selected as a programming language for this book and you may also be surprised, if you know JS, why I don't use the operator `new` and classes introduced in ES6. I did it on purpose; it's not a mistake. First of all, I believe that JavaScript is a perfect language to demonstrate how key OO concepts work. Second, I think that classes are not needed in OOP—just objects are enough.

Let me interrupt you and remind that the code you see in this book can be found in `yegor256/jo` GitHub repository. Clone it to your laptop (more about it in the Section 3.1):

```
$ git clone https://github.com/yegor256/jo
$ cd jo
```

Then, list all the tags available:

```
$ git tag
```

You will see the list of tags related to the sections in the book. Pick one of them and check it out, for example:

```
$ git checkout 3.mock
```

If you find any bugs there, don't hesitate to submit an issue or, even better, a pull request.

2.1 Indentation

Let's draw the field where all of the game elements will live. This is how your `game.html` file should look (we've had `a.html` and now it's time to create another one; I'm sure you can do it):

```
<!DOCTYPE html>
<html>
  <head>
    <title>Space Invaders</title>
  </head>
  <body>
    <section id="field"/>
  </body>
</html>
```

You already know the syntax of HTML, which mostly consists of *tags* and *attributes*. `<html>` is a tag, which includes the `<head>` tag, which includes the `<title>` tag. This multi-level nesting structure is pretty typical for many programming languages. You will meet it in many places. Many years ago, to make this nesting more visible on the screen, programmers invented *indentation*:

```
<html>
  <body>
    <section id="field"/>
```

Every subsequent level of nesting is shifted to the right by a number of spaces. Actually, many years ago, a tabulation symbol was originally used. However, it's now considered a rudiment, which is never used in the source code. But you still use the `tab` key on your keyboard to shift the next line right. You don't click ⬜ +⬜; you just hit `tab` and your text editor understands you. Any modern IDE will understand you, for sure. I'm using Sublime Text right now and it does this shifting perfectly. Moreover, when I want to get back to the previous level of indentation, I just hit `delete` and the cursor jumps to the left by two positions.

Some programmers, however, don't pay enough attention to the formatting of their code and don't indent it correctly. You may see this code very often:

```
<!DOCTYPE html>
<html><head>
<title>Space Invaders</title></head>
<body>
    <section id="field"/>
</body></html>
```

This is the exact same code and Safari will understand it just as well as the one above, but it's not formatted correctly. When such code is in front of you, you should reformat it before you start working with it. A correctly intended program is much more readable that the one without indentation, or with incorrectly indented elements (which is even worse than no indentation at all). The code, if it's written correctly, should always resemble a *ladder* with multiple steps, going left and right. This, for example, is a piece of code I was working with just a few days ago; it's in Java:

```
String def = Charset.defaultCharset().name();
if (!"UTF-8".equals(def)) {
  throw new IllegalStateException(
    String.format(
      "Default encoding is %s",
      Charset.defaultCharset()
    )
  );
}
return new TkSslOnly(
  new TkWithHeaders(
    new TkVersioned(
      new TkMeasured(
        new TkGzip(
          new TkFlash(
            new TkAppFallback(
              new TkAppAuth(
                new TkForward(
                  TkApp.regex(base)
                )
              )
            )
          )
        )
      )
    )
  ),
    String.format("X-Revision: %s", REV),
    "Vary: Cookie"
  )
);
```

You may not understand the code or like the prefixed naming convention used for these Java classes, but you can certainly see the levels of abstraction. You see what stays on top of everything and what is nested way deeper, and that's why it's less high-level and more detailed.

There is a simple rule of indentation that I use and recommend you to use too: the position where you start an element should be the position where you close it. For example:

```
<html>
  <body>
    <section id="field"/>
```

Where do I close the `<body>` tag? What is the right position for it? Let me give you a few options and you tell me which one obeys the rule just announced:

```
<!-- Option A: -->
<html>
  <body>
    <section id="field"/>
  </body>
<!-- Option B: -->
<html>
  <body>
    <section id="field"/>
</body>
<!-- Option C: -->
<html>
  <body>
    <section id="field"/></body>
```

None of them. Option A closed the `<body>` tag at the same indentation level as `<section>`, which is wrong. It confuses the reader. Option B closes too far left, at the level of `<html>`, again confusing the reader. Option C is also incorrect since the indentation level of `</body>` is so far right that it will be very hard to find it there. This is the correct formatting:

```
<html>
  <body>
    <section id="field"/>
  </body>
```

Most IDEs and text editors will draw vertical lines to help you visually connect elements at the same indentation level. Pay attention to those lines, and make sure you satisfy their expectations.

Visually obvious and elegant indentation is a very important quality of clean source code. If you don't see a ladder, your code is probably bad.

By the way, many years ago, most programmers were *indenting* by eight space characters (or one tab character, which was 8-spaces wide). Then, four spaces became a standard de facto. Now, it seems, two characters are enough. I recommend you use two characters in all of your programs, no matter what the programming language is.

★
Why was tabulation originally eight spaces?

★ ★
Reformat the HTML code above so that it takes less than six lines, keeping the indentation consistent.

★ ★
In your editor, find a way to reformat the code with a single click (a.k.a. auto-format).

★ ★
Explain what `Charset.defaultCharset()` is about. Name five of the most popular charsets and explain how they work.

★ ★
Read *Code Complete (2004)* by McConnell [15].

★ ★ ★
Explain the difference between UTF-8 and UTF-16.

2.2 Console

Remember when we discussed runtime environments and the way the computer interprets commands in a programming language? The command line, which you use to tell your operating system that you want to copy a file or open an HTML file in Safari, is an interface to the operating system, also known as a *shell*. The shell interprets you when you say `ls` and returns the list of files and sub-directories in the current directory.

There are two ways of interacting with a runtime environment: interactive and non-interactive. The shell in the command line is the interactive way. You type something in, hit `return`, and see the result immediately. You need something else, type in the next command, and get the result. To the contrary, Safari is a non-interactive runtime: you create an HTML file, open it in Safari, which reads your *entire* program and executes it. You can't do anything in the middle of this process. You just wait and see the result of the entire set of commands. You don't say to Safari, "Hey, render `greet` for me," and then "Now render `<b>World</b>`." You just give it the entire program and see how it manages to interpret it and show you the result.

This difference is important. Modern programming languages and their runtime environments, like Safari for HTML, are mostly non-interactive. They expect you to provide a file with a program, then they will interpret and execute it. But it wasn't like that before. When I was a kid writing that Basic program, I had to do it like this.

First, right after my computer with MS-DOS, an operating system developed by Microsoft, was *booted up*, I would say to the command line: `gwbasic` and then `return`. GW-Basic, a runtime

56

environment developed by Microsoft, started and asked me for the next command. I would say `10 INPUT X` and then the interpreter would confirm that the line 10 now had the command `INPUT X`. Let me show you the entire script, and you will understand what was going on[1]:

```
C:\>gwbasic
GW-BASIC 3.23
(C) Copyright Microsoft 1983,1984,1985,1986,1987,1988
60890 Bytes free
Ok
10 INPUT X
20 PRINT "You just entered", X
RUN
? 256
You just entered 256
Ok
```

This is what's going on here. First, the shell of the MS-DOS says `C:\>` and expects me to provide the command. I say `gwbasic` and the GW-Basic interpreter starts. It prints some copyright information, then says how many bytes I have in memory, and then says `Ok`. This is its *prompt*. Every interpreter has something like this: a short piece of text it gives you when it's ready to accept your next command. In all interpreters, you will see a blinking cursor staying right after the prompt.

Next, I say `10 INPUT X` and hit `return`. GW-Basic consumes my command and interprets it as: "The code at the line 10 must contain `INPUT X`, no matter what it contained before." Then I say `20 PRINT ...` and the line by the number 20 is saved. These lines are not executed yet; they are just being recorded in memory. Only when I say `RUN` does the code get executed and

---

[1] You may want to try it yourself at gw-basic.com.

print `?`, expecting me to "input" a number. When I enter 256 and hit `return`, the line 20 prints something back to me, and the execution of my small program finishes. GW-Basic says `Ok` again, expecting me to instruct it what to do next. You can play with it, if you manage to find its simulator online. Or you can even download a modern version of it for your laptop.

I demonstrated this rudiment piece of software in order to show the difference between interpreters, like command line shell or GW-Basic, and runtime environments, which take your program as a whole piece and run it, like Safari.

However, many runtime environments—including Safari—still provide us programmers the ability to talk to them through a *console*, accepting commands one by one. Console is yet another name for a command line, in addition to shell, command prompt, terminal, and maybe some others. Let's check how the console of Safari works, which is a part of their *Web Inspector* tool set. I won't explain how to enable it in Safari first or how to get into the console; find it out yourself on Google. When you are ready and you see a blinking cursor, type: `2 + 2`. Safari will understand you and will print the result of this simple arithmetic calculation.

The language you just used was JavaScript.

★
What does CLI stand for?

★★
Name five programming languages that have both interpreters and *compilers*.

2.3 Object

Now, the most interesting and important part of this book. We will talk about objects, which are the core idea of object-oriented programming. No matter what the programming language of your choice in the future will be—provided it will be object-oriented—you will deal with objects. There are other types of languages and so called programming *paradigms*, including functional and logical. There is also procedural programming, which GW-Basic, for example, is about. In this book, we are not interested in them at all. We study OOP.

OOP is not so complex, to be honest. However ... You know what Edsger W. Dijkstra, one of the most famous computer scientists, said about it in 1989? He said that "object-oriented programming is an exceptionally bad idea which could only have originated in California." You know what Paul Graham, one of the founders of Y Combinator, said about it in 2003? He said that "object-oriented programming offers a sustainable way to write spaghetti code." I think that the most accurate summary was given by Alan Kay, the author of the object-oriented idea. He said in 1997: "I invented the term object-oriented, and I can tell you I did not have C++ in mind."

I agree with them all. The object-orientation and the idea of an *object* is way simpler and elegant than what all existing object-oriented languages implement. There are many things in those languages, including JavaScript (which we will start using in a few pages), that are not necessary, or too complex, or simply wrong. We will not even discuss them. We will focus on what is right and what are the true object-oriented concepts. The object is one of them; the main one.

So, the object.

Open the `game.html` file in Safari. Go to the JavaScript console, where you were entering `2 + 2` and write this: `document.write("Hello!")`. See what happens?

Here, the `document` is an object. The `write()` is one of its *methods*. The `"Hello!"` is the *argument* of the method. You just had a conversation with an object by the name `document`. You asked *him* to write something for you on the page. You told him specifically what you wanted him to write for you. And he did what you asked. He found the page and decided which pixels have to become black to make this `"Hello!"` visible the way you want it. He knew how to talk to the page so that the page would understand him. She, the page, did everything he asked her to do and he returned back the result to you, which you can see in the console. It is `undefined`, if I'm not mistaken.

I'm anthropomorphizing objects (calling them "he" and "she") to make it clear that an object is a pretty smart thing that must be respected. The only right way of dealing with an object is a polite conversation just like we just did, via its methods. We ask, they work for us.

★
Find five more popular quotes about OOP.

★ ★
Study the history of OOP and explain why it was invented.

★ ★
Name 10 of the most popular OOP languages and compare them using pros and cons.

★ ★
Read my blog post: *Who Is an Object? (2016)*.

2.4 Name

An object has a name; the `document` is the name. Object names can be pretty short, like `file`, `document`, or `window`, or long and *compound*, like `white_rabbit`, `simpleTextFile`, or `SUPER_SECRET_PASSWORD`. Different programming languages have different *naming conventions* for their objects. For example, in C++ compound object names usually consist of lower case words separated by an underscore, like `free_memory` or `words_in_file`. In Java and JavaScript there is "camel case" notation, where words are *concatenated* and all of them—except the first one—are capitalized, like `renderedPixels` or `bytesAvailable`.

No matter what the convention is, I would recommend you name your objects as one-word *nouns*. Compound names (also known as *qualified* names) are considered *bad practice* in programming, not only by myself, but some other authors, as well. The `document` is a perfect object name, while `my_document` is not as perfect or even simply bad. Why do programmers give their objects compound names? First of all, in order to make it obvious what the object really means and does. If you have many "documents" and they all are *visible*, you have to find a way to introduce some distinction between them. The `my_` prefix could play a role in such a distinction.

Many years ago, when computers were slow and the amount of symbols you had to type to write a program mattered, programmers were naming their *variables* with a single letter, like I did in the Basic program above: `X`, `Y`, or `i`. When too many objects were visible at the same time and there were not enough letters in English, numeric suffixes were used, like `X1`, or `i3`. Needless to say, it was rather difficult to read programs when objects that were *visible* together were named like `i`, `i2`, and `i3`.

Now, the amount of symbols required to write a program doesn't really matter. Some programmers believe that the longer the name, the higher the readability of the program. To some extent, they're right. Take a look at our HTML program again:

`Hello, <b>world</b>`

Wouldn't it be more readable if instead of `<b>`, we used something like this:

`Hello, <bold>world</bold>`

Better, right? Yes, but longer. For HTML programs, the length matters because each `.html` file may eventually be transferred over the Internet, and the larger it is, the longer the user will have to wait. But for JavaScript, it's not as important. It's not at all important for Java and C++. What matters in modern languages is readability of the code. Too short names, like `i` or `<b>`, definitely decrease readability unless they are very obvious and the *scope of visibility* is rather small. Excessively long names, like `best_option_at_the_moment`, create the illusion of better readability, but conceal the real problem: too big of a visibility scope.

★ ★

Explain how Hungarian notation works.

★ ★

Find out which authors are also against compound names and which are in favor of them, and compare their arguments.

★ ★

Go to `www.google.com`. Using Web Inspector in your browser, check how many documents were downloaded to your laptop.

★ ★

Read my blog post: *A Compound Name Is a Code Smell (2015)*.

2.5 Visibility

Now it's time to explain what *object visibility*, means and what the *scope* of it iss. Look at this piece of JavaScript code:

```
const names = ["Jeffrey", "Walter", "Bonny"];
names.forEach(function(name) {
   console.log("Hello, " + name);
});
```

It's a *loop* that takes an *array* of names and calls the same *anonymous function*, passing each of them as its single *argument*. The function *logs* a greeting message to the console that includes the name provided as an argument. Too many new words? Don't worry, they're not important for now, but we will get back to all of them later. What's important here is the *indentation* of the line with `console.log`:

```
// Prepare a list of names
// Take one of them and call it "name"
  console.log("Hello, " + name);
// Forget it and take the next one
```

We *iterate* through names and do the same operation over and over again, each time calling the next `name`. On each iteration, `name` means something different to us; every time it's a new thing. First, it's "Jeffrey," then it's "Walter," and finally it's "Bonny."

What do you think happens if we start working with the `name` after this block of code:

```
const names = ["Jeffrey", "Walter", "Bonny"];
names.forEach(function(name) {
  console.log("Hello, " + name);
});
console.log("Bye, " + name); // Error!
```

There will be an error at this new line because the scope of visibility of `name` is over. The *variable* `name` is only visible inside the function, and is not visible outside of it. To emphasize this fact, we indent right the all of the code of the function. Every time we indent right, a new scope of visibility starts. When we indent back left, the scope ends. Everything that existed inside the scope is forgotten when the scope ends. Everything that is visible in a larger scope is also visible in all scopes it *includes*. For example, this code is valid:

```
const names = ["Jeffrey", "Walter", "Bonny"];
names.forEach(function(name) {
  console.log(
    "There are " + names.length + " friends"
  );
});
```

We *refer* to the variable `names` from the scope, which is included. I'm not sure whether it's totally legal to say *include* here, but it seems to be the right word for me. Large scopes indeed include smaller ones. You may also hear people saying that scopes are *nested* into each other.

Imagine a house with a few rooms. You enter the house and your name is Jessica. We meet you in the lobby and call you by your name: Jessica. Then, there is a room with some other people inside. They are sitting there and waiting for a poet to enter. You enter the room and they all call you "poet". They have no idea that you are Jessica; you are a poet to them. You read them a few poems and leave the room. Now you are Jessica again. We don't know anything about what happened in that room and we don't know that you were called a "poet" in there. It was a *local* story for you and those people in the room. For us, in the lobby, it's of no interest.

★ ★
Explain the difference between arrays, sets, queues, and lists.

★ ★
Read my blog post: *How Data Visibility Hurts Maintainability (2019)*.

2.6 Variable

The "poet" was your *nickname* in the room. But you were still the same Jessica. You were the same person because Jessica is also a nickname, but with a larger scope of visibility. Programmers call these nicknames *variables*. The `name` was a variable.

Any human being may have many nicknames: Jessica, poet, teacher, you, the-lady-in-a-white-blouse. Any *object* may have many variables referring to it: `name`, `i`, `name_of_friend`, etc. The object remains the same, while its names may change.

In JavaScript, new variables are *declared* using the word `const`, just like we did with the variable `names`:

```
const names = ["Jeffrey", "Walter", "Bonny"];
```

We just told our JavaScript runtime: create a new object, an array of three strings, and call it `names`. We can declare a new variable with a new name and make it refer to the same object:

```
const friends = names;
```

If you check what is in `friends` and you will see ....

Wait a minute, how do you check it? Let's pause for a minute, install and try a *headless* JavaScript runtime, which basically is not a browser (hence why it's "headless"). You need Node.js. Install it and try this from your command line:

```
$ node
> const names = ["Jeffrey", "Walter", "Bonny"]
undefined
> names
[ 'Jeffrey', 'Walter', 'Bonny' ]
> const friends = names
undefined
> friends
[ 'Jeffrey', 'Walter', 'Bonny' ]
> friends.push("Maude")
4
```

We just created a new object and a variable `names`, which is referring to it. Then, we created another variable `friends`, which refers to the variable `names`, which refers to the object. At the end, we added a new string to the object and Node.js said `4`, which is the size of the array. There were three names in `friends` and now there are four. Let's check how many strings are in the `names` array:

```
> names
[ 'Jeffrey', 'Walter', 'Bonny', 'Maude' ]
```

As you can see, the modifications we did with the object `friends` were automatically applied to the object `names`. Actually, there were no two objects; there is only one object. There are two nicknames.

JavaScript, just like many other languages, including Java and C#, has an exception of this simple principle. Not all objects may have many nicknames, known as variables. Some objects may only be referred to by a single variable. They are objects of *primitive types*: numbers, for example. Take a look at this:

```
> const price = 50
undefined
> const cost = price
undefined
> cost = 10
10
> price
50
```

When we do `const cost = price`, a new object is created (a *copy* of the existing one) and a new variable `cost` refers to it. Why JavaScript designers decided to do it this way, I don't know. My best bet is on their lack of understanding of the philosophy of object-oriented programming. You just have to remember that objects of certain *types* can't have multiple variables and will always be *cloned* when you attempt to give them new names.

★
Our code says `"Jeffrey"` (in double quotes), but Node.js prints `'Jeffrey'` (in single quotes). Why?

★★
What is a *constant*? Explain the difference between a variable and a constant.

★★
Explain what *circular references* are.

★★
Explain why Node.js sometimes says `undefined` in the snippets above.

★★
Try to install another headless JavaScript runtime environment. Which one works for you, and what makes it better or worse than Node.js?

2.7 Type

Any object has a *type*. Some programming languages—instead of "types"—say "classes," or "interfaces," or "protocols," or even "prototypes." There are many names, but the idea is always the same: If "Jessica" is a variable and "you" are an object, than "human" is a type. In other words, Jessica is a nickname of an object of type human. Or people.

All objects of type human are *expected* to have similar behavior. They all walk, talk, drink, and sleep. There are also subtypes, like men and women, for example. Women can do some things men can't, like carry a child. People is a supertype of women and men. There is also a supertype that humans belong to: living organisms. All types in any programming language constitute a type hierarchy. You can create your own types, finding the right type to subtype from.

The object `50` is of type `Number`. You can check it:

```
> const price = 50
undefined
> typeof price
'number'
```

The object `"Jeffrey"` is of type `String`:

```
> const name = "Jeffrey"
undefined
> typeof name
'string'
```

A better way to say is: the object `"Jeffrey"` *is a* `String`.

You may ask, what are types for? They exist to help us *decouple* declaration and implementation. Here is what it means in simple words: when you buy a car, it either has two pedals, or three and a stick. The first one is of type "automatic"; the second one is of type "manual." This is the *declaration* of its features. Each type of car has its own declaration. You either push the gas pedal and it goes forward, or you push the clutch and then the gas, and then you release the clutch, and so on. There are two different protocols for interaction with the car. They are declared and you know how to work with each of them. Your driving habits are *coupled* with one or both of them if you know how to drive a car with a manual transmission. Kids don't have this *coupling*, which is why they go to driving schools: to learn how to use one of those protocols.

On the other hand, there are many car manufacturers on the market, like Ford, Mercedes-Benz, BMW, and many others. They all make their cars to work exactly as you'd expect them to, according to one of those protocols. Ferrari, no matter how creative its designers could be, will still have two pedals and the right one will push the car forward. However, the way Ferrari transforms that pedal into moving forward and how Tesla does it are two different *implementations* of the same *interface*. When you buy Tesla, you don't want to change your habits and start hitting the left pedal in order to make the car move. You want your Tesla to behave exactly (or very close to) how you were taught to use all cars in your driving school. You want to be *decoupled* from the implementation details.

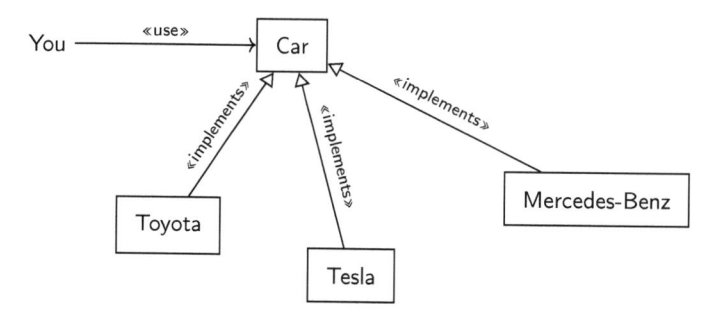

Figure 2.1: UML Type Diagram of Cars

Imagine what would happen if each car maker improvised and created a totally different interface for their cars. Mercedes-Benz would have four pedals, Citroën would expect you to hit the gas with your left hand, and Mazda would ask you to show turn signals using the middle pedal. It's very likely that most of their decisions would make sense, but for end-users, such a variety of differences between implementations would only cause one thing to happen: they would stop buying different cars and be stuck with just one maker or even one model. That would be a disaster for everybody—car buyers and car makers. Maybe something like that was happening a hundred years ago, when the automobile industry was still very young.

To avoid such a chaos, any mature industry introduces *standards* and invites all product makers to obey them. And if they don't obey and create something non-standard and unique, they risk losing the market. Nobody wants to be attached to a single implementation because this only makes our lives harder. What will we do when BMW stops making cars we are used to driving, or their cars become too expensive, or Toyota makes a car that is better looking and cheaper? We will have to go to driving school again and learn how to the use pedals and buttons in a new Toyota? Sounds like a bad plan.

Moreover, if an industry has formal standards, any new company can simply download them and create a new car that the market will immediately buy if it's cheaper than others. In the automobile industry, this may not be the case since drivers are coupled with implementation and many of them need more than just a vehicle. They want the brand, the color, the style, the driving experience, and so on. But if we look at, for example, the industry of micro-electronics, this statement is true. If a company creates a new microchip that works according to the standard, nobody will care about its maker or how it's implemented inside.

In object-oriented programming, the situation is exactly the same. We don't want to be coupled with a single specific implementation of an object created by, say, Robert, a programmer from our Santa Cruz office. Such a coupling will expose us to many risks. What if Robert leaves the company and nobody else is interested in supporting the code he wrote? What if we find out that Robert's code isn't perfect and there are better solutions to the same problem? What if Robert gets too creative and starts making frequent changes to the object? Will we have to catch up every week and change our code too, in order to be *compatible* with what Robert is doing?

Nope, we don't want any of that. We want a standard to stay between us and Robert. We want Robert to do what the standard is saying and never bother us with the implementation details. We don't care about them. We just want to follow the rules, do what the protocol requires, and feel safe.

A type in object-oriented programming is the standard, the protocol, the set of rules, the definition of the interface, or the contract between objects. Without types, we would be in a big mess, having many *ad hoc* relationships between objects.

Remember how we did this just a few pages ago:

`friends.push("Maude")`

The `friends` object was of type `Array` and we called its method `push` with a single argument `"Maude"`. The object `friends` understood our call and added a new string to itself. Do we know how this method `push()` is implemented in this object? No. Do we want to know? Not at all. We just want the object to do what we expect of an object of type `Array`: add strings to itself when `push()` is called.

There is one more thing you need to know about types. Imagine you go to the dealer to buy a car. There could be two scenarios. The first one: you ask for an automatic transmission and if they give you a manual one, you just don't buy. The second one: they give you whatever they have, you pay and then figure out how to drive it on your way home. The first scenario is called *strong typing*. The second one is *weak typing*.

Some programming languages are strongly typed and won't allow anyone to give you any objects unless they are exactly the types you ask for. If you ask for an `Array`, they give you an `Array`. If they don't, the compiler of the language itself complains with a *compile error*. Java works like this.

Some other languages are weakly typed. You can't even tell them what type of object you expect. JavaScript, which we will use in this book, is unfortunately one of those languages. This is perfectly legal JavaScript code:

```
const friends = 123;
friends.push("Maude");
```

The object `friends` of type `Number` doesn't have method

`push()`, as you can imagine. However, this program will start, execute, and only fail when the method `push()` is called, when it will be too late. Moreover, we can do this:

```
const friends = {
  push: function(name) {
    console.log("Oops, sorry!");
  }
};
friends.push("Maude");
```

Here, we create a new object `friends` of our own anonymous type, which has no name. The object has a single method `push`, which, as you can see, doesn't do anything useful, but prints a message to the console log. The next line, where `.push("Maude")` is called, will not know that `friends` is not an `Array`. It will think that it's an `Array` because it *behaves* like an `Array`. This is called *duck typing*. If it walks like a duck and it quacks like a duck, then it must be a duck, as the saying goes.

Duck typing (or weak typing) makes programming faster. You don't need to think about types, you can just call whatever methods you like and nobody will complain. Until they start complaining in production, when your code is already in front of the user and it's too late to say "Sorry"! I would even put it this way: Weak typing is for weak programmers, strong typing is for strong programmers.

★
Some lines of the code above end with semi-colons, while others don't. Why?

★ ★

Explain the difference between strong/weak and static/dynamic typing dichotomies.

★ ★

Compare JavaScript and TypeScript and identify their pros and cons.

★ ★

Explain why most OOP books say that you should prefer composition over inheritance.

★ ★

Explain the difference between subtyping and implementation inheritance.

2.8 Method

You probably already understand that objects have methods that can be called with a number of arguments, like we just did with the method `push`:

```
friends.push("Maude");
```

Here, `friends` is the object, `push` is the name of the method, and `"Maude"` is the argument. There could be as many arguments as the method expects us to provide. When the method is *declared*, it defines how many arguments are expected and what their names *inside* the *visibility scope* of the method's body will be:

```
const lucy = {
  greet: function(name, locale) {
    if (locale == "fr") {
      console.log("Bonjour, " + name);
    } else {
      console.log("Hello, " + name);
    }
  }
};
```

Here, the method `greet` of the object `lucy` expects two arguments: `name` and `locale`, and they are part of the method *signature*—this is how a one line declaration of the method is called, without its body:

```
greet: function(name, locale)
```

In JavaScript, the signature has a name and a list of *parameters*. In other languages, it may also include the type of the object this method *returns*, or even a few objects. It may also include types of exceptions this method may *throw*, and maybe some other things. It doesn't really matter. What matters is that a method has a signature and the body. The signature is just like a type; it's a *contract* between those who call the method and those who implement the method. The callers don't want to know what's inside. They just provide *input* arguments and expect something as an *output*.

The method `greet` doesn't return anything. It just salutes the user in the console, using user's name and the locale the user speaks in. Methods can call each other, for example:

```
const lucy = {
  greet: function(name, locale) {
    console.log(this.greeting(name, locale));
  },
  greeting: function(n, lang) {
    const text;
    if (lang == "fr") {
      text = "Bonjour, " + n;
    } else {
      text = "Hello, " + n;
    }
    return text;
  }
};
```

The method `greet` calls the method `greeting`, passing two arguments into it. Inside the body of the method `greet`, the name of the user is called `name`, but inside the `greeting` it's called `n`. The `locale` also changes its name to `lang`.

★
There is a double `==` operator between `locale` and `"fr"`. Why not a single one?

★
What is the difference between parameters and arguments of a method?

★ ★
What is the object that the variable `text` refers to, right after this line: `const text;` ?

★ ★
What happens if we pass one or three arguments to the method `greeting()` instead of two?

★ ★ ★
Create a JavaScript object `fibonacci` with a method `calculate` that will accept a single argument `n` and return the *n*-th Fibonacci number. Use *recursion*.

2.9 Operator

You certainly noticed that aside from method calling via *dot notation*, like `lucy.greet()` or `this.greeting()`, our code has yet another mechanism of interacting with objects, which is known as *operators*:

`text = "Bonjour, " + n;`

Here, we have two objects: `"Bonjour, "` and `n`. To create a new object, we *concatenate* them. What happens is that we ask the first object to *add* the second one to it, and formally it would look like this:

`text = "Bonjour, ".concatenate(n);`

But to make *some* operations more convenient and less verbose, operators were invented. Technically, they were invented long before object-oriented programming was invented, but in a pure object-oriented world, operators are just *shortcuts* for method calls. The object of type `String` has method `concatenate()` and JavaScript runtime knows that when a programmer says `+`, it's time to call exactly that method.

You've seen other operators above in this book. For example, `==` is also an operator, and this code:

```
if (lang == "fr") {
```

more formally would look like this:

```
if (lang.equals("fr")) {
```

There are mostly *unary* and *binary* operators. The `==` operator is binary since it needs two parties: the left and the right. `+` is also binary. However, there are unary operators in some languages, too. For example, in JavaScript you can do this with an object of type `Number`:

```
x++;
```

This unary operator `++` is a shortcut for:

```
x.add(1);
```

Remember that all operators are shortcuts for good old object methods. There is only one exception, the *assignment* operator: `x = 1`. It can't be converted to a method of an object because there is no object on the left side. There is a variable, which is going to refer to a new object, but the object it was referring to before is gone.

★
Name all of the operators that exist in JavaScript.

★
What does `this` stand for in JavaScript?

★ ★
There is also the `===` operator in JavaScript. How does it work and how is it different from `==`?

2.10 Statement

Actually, I'm wrong about the assignment. It's not an operator; it's a *statement*. A statement is an instruction to the language interpreter, which doesn't touch objects:

```
const lucy = {
  name: function() {
    return "Lucy";
  }
};
```

Speaking honestly, I don't know how many statements are in this code. Most likely four. The first one is the *variable declaration* statement, which starts with the `const` keyword, and can formally be specified by this Backus-Naur Form (BNF):

```
<variable_declaration> :=
    "const" <name> "=" <object_declaration> ";"
```

The *object declaration* is the one that starts with a curly bracket and ends with it:

```
<object_declaration> :=
    "{" <method_declaration>* "}"
```

The *method declaration* has a name, a colon and a function:

```
<method_declaration> :=
    <name> ":" "function" "(" <argument>* ")"
    "{" <method_body> "}"
```

And there is also a `return` *statement*, which basically starts with `return` and ends with the object that has to be returned.

What we just did is also known as a *syntax analysis*. We broke down the JavaScript language into lexems and formally defined the syntax of the language. Of course, the real syntax

80

specification is much more complex and involves many more statements and keywords, but that's how those programmers who create new languages start.

★
Explain who invented the BNF and what for.

★★
Explain how `if`, `for`, `switch`, and `while` statements work in JavaScript.

★★
Define `<argument>` using the same Backus-Naur form.

2.11 Constructor

Take a look at this code once again:

```
const lucy = {
  greet: function(name, locale) {
    const text;
    if (locale == "fr") {
      text = "Bonjour, " + name;
    } else {
      text = "Hello, " + name;
    }
    console.log(text);
  }
};
```

It's a single object `lucy`, which is able to say hello in two different languages. What if we want to have many objects that

are able to say hello in different languages? And we want to have
an ability to *configure* them. Say I have this conversation
protocol for my objects:

`en` Hello, Jeff!
`fr` Bonjour, Nicolas!
`ru` Привет, Петр!

We don't want to create three different objects, writing their code
over and over again with a slight modification to the `greet`
method. We want to have an ability to *construct* them by
specifying the arguments they will *encapsulate* and use later,
when the time comes. Here is how:

```
function doorman(t) {
  return {
    text: t,
    greet: function(name) {
      console.log(
        this.text.replace(/\{name\}/, name)
      );
    }
  };
}
```

Now, we *instantiate* `lucy`:

```
const lucy = doorman("Bonjour, {name}!");
```

Then, we call the `greet` method:

```
> lucy.greet("Nicolas")
Bonjour, Nicolas!
```

We can instantiate as many objects as we like, making each of
them encapsulate text with the `{name}` *placeholder*:

```
const lucy = doorman("Bonjour, {name}!");
const john = doorman("Hello, {name}!");
const anna = doorman("Привет, {name}!");
```

The `doorman` is a *constructor* that builds *new* objects. All it does is make an object and return it. It doesn't do anything else and doesn't have any other statements except the `return` one that returns the object.

★ ★

Explain how operator `new` works in JavaScript.

★ ★

Rewrite the `doorman` code above using ES6 JavaScript classes.

★ ★

A few pages above, the method `replace` of type `String` accepted `/{name}/` as its first argument. It was a *regular expression*. In its current version it only replaces `{name}` placeholders, but doesn't replace, for example, `{NAME}`. Modify it to make it *case insensitive*.

★ ★ ★

Explain how *look ahead* works in regular expressions.

2.12 Attribute

The argument of the `doorman` constructor was *encapsulated* in the `text` *attribute* of a new object:

```
function doorman(t) {
  return {
    text: t
  };
}
```

The `text` is only visible inside the methods of the object and is a nickname for the object provided as an argument. Of course, in this particular case, the object `t` is copied (because it's of a primitive type), but in all other cases, an attribute, just like any other variable, would be a nickname for an existing object.

An object may have as many attributes as possible, but it seems reasonable to have a rather limited number of them in any object: between one and four. If there are more, something is not right with the object; it's too large. If there are none, the object is not configurable and most likely too small.

The object we just instantiated can become an argument for a constructor of another object. For example:

```
function entrance(d) {
  return {
    doorman: d,
    enter: function(friends) {
      friends.forEach(function(name) {
        this.doorman.greet(name);
      }.bind(this));
    }
  };
}
```

Now, we have to instantiate the doorman first:

```
const lucy = doorman("Bonjour, {name}!");
```

And then create a `door`:

```
const door = entrance(lucy);
```

Then, we just call:

```
door.enter(["Jeff", "Judy", "Sarah"]);
```

And `lucy` will receive three consecutive calls to its method `greet`.

Then, we can create an even larger object that will encapsulate the `door` and let people enter it, but the list of people will be retrieved from the database. For example:

```
function vault(s, e) {
  return {
    storage: s,
    entrance: e,
    open: function() {
      const users = this.storage.whoCanEnter();
      this.entrance.enter(users);
      console.log(users.length + " users are in!");
    }
  };
}
```

Then, we create an *anonymous* object `vault` and call its method `open`:

```
vault(storage, door).open();
```

We can do this *object composition* in one statement:

```
vault(
  storage, // Created somewhere else
  entrance(
    doorman("Bonjour, {name}!")
  )
).open();
```

85

In this statement, we create an anonymous object `doorman`, pass it as an argument to the anonymous object `entrance`, which is then passed as an argument to the anonymous object `vault`, which gets a call at `open`.

An object can't live without its *dependencies*, also known as attributes. If we let our objects only work with what they receive as arguments of their methods, they will be very difficult to manage. We will always have to remember what we have to pass to their methods and to keep those other supplementary objects close by. Objects were invented mostly to *minimize* the amount of data we have to transfer between our statements and remember what we did. Once we encapsulate something in an object, it stays there forever and we don't need to remember it anymore.

Look at the object `lucy`. We encapsulate the text there and then we only have to deal with `lucy`, completely forgetting what is encapsulated inside. We just call `lucy.greet("Jeff")` and everything else happens automatically because `lucy` knows what to do. This technique is also known as *information hiding*. `lucy` knows something, but those who communicate with `lucy` have no idea what's there. They *trust* `lucy`.

To be honest, looking back at my experience of writing code for about thirty years, I can say that most code maintenance problems come from our inability to keep all of the important concepts, ideas, and data in our heads. Simply put, we forget things. Once we forget, we start making mistakes and the code gets messy. Eventually, we can't even remember what the code, which we were writing a few days ago, is supposed to do. And we have to rewrite it from scratch. This is the ultimate outcome of the maintainability issues we discussed before.

Code that is difficult to maintain is the worst code. It's not the one that's slow. No! It's not the one that doesn't do what is expected and has *bugs*. No! It's not the one that's too complex. No! The worst code is the kind we can't easily and *inexpensively* modify. The main expense here, as you understand, is *us programmers*. The time we invest in writing the code is the primary cost factor in the software business. The longer we need to stare at the code before we can start modifying it, the worse the programmer who wrote it is. We don't want to be those programmers. We want to write code that anyone will be able to read and modify quickly, including ourselves.

Encapsulating dependencies inside objects is the first and main step towards maintainability of the code, and it's not an easy task. Actually, the most complex task in object-oriented programming is deciding what exactly will be encapsulated and what the objects that encapsulate what will be. In our simple examples above, I made those decisions in just a few minutes because there are just a few objects and they're all far from real world. Still, I was making hard choices: `doorman` vs. `waiter`, `jenkins`, and `steward`; `entrance` vs. `house`, `home`, `main`, `team`; and so on. I picked `doorman` and `entrance`. Maybe it was not the best choice, but I had to make some.

In a real software package, it usually takes hours and sometimes even days to decide what objects we should have and what their names will be. And, of course, who will encapsulate who. Don't expect it to be easy and try to enjoy this process of *inventing* objects.

We will have to invent some of them a bit later to create a web game. In your real projects, you will have to invent many more of them. It won't often be easy and you'll want to make compromises: you won't like the names, but you'll have to move on and you'll tolerate your imperfect choices. Don't do that. Unless you are completely happy with how your objects are named and what they encapsulate, don't start writing code. Constructing and then *wiring* objects together is the most important process in object-oriented programming.

★

Why do you think I name constructor arguments as `d` and `e`, while attribute names are `doorman` and `entrance`? Is it possible to give them both the same name (for example, the argument `doorman` and the attribute `doorman`)?

★

What exactly is an anonymous object?

★★

Define a similar `doorman` constructor in Java, Ruby, Python, and C#. Then, instantiate a few objects in each of these languages, using this one-argument constructor. Which of them do you like the most, syntax wise?

★★

Explain what *Dependency Injection* and *Inversion of Control* are. Where in the code above have we used them?

★★

Get rid of `bind(this)` and make sure the code still works.

★★★

The object created by the constructor `vault` has no name. Is it possible to call method `open` twice at this very object? If it's not possible now, what can we do to make it possible without giving it a name?

2.13 Exception

Take a look at this code one more time:

```
greeting: function(n, lang) {
  const text;
  if (lang == "fr") {
    text = "Bonjour, " + n;
  } else {
    text = "Hello, " + n;
  }
  return text;
}
```

See what happens if we call it with the `"ru"` locale:

```
> greeting("Петр", "ru")
Hello, Петр
```

Not exactly what good software should do. Good software should always try to be overprotective against use cases that are not expected. A method should not start working unless it gets the arguments that perfectly fit its intended use. For example, an ideal implementation of the method `greeting` must *reject* these calls, because they are too suspicious or just wrong:

```
greeting("John", "")      // The locale is empty
greeting("", "en")        // The name is empty
greeting("*&%L$J)1", "en") // The name is not a name
greeting("Sarah", "!!!")  // The locale is not a locale
```

And so on.

Some programmers preach an opposite philosophy. They believe that a method must do everything possible to *not fail*, no matter how much garbage is coming in. Their philosophy is called Fail Safe because the code they write will almost never fail. This may

89

seem like a good approach at first sight. However, it will only hurt the maintainability of the code in the long run. Here is why.

If our code doesn't complain about the `"!!!"` locale and pretends that it is English or something else, it will work, but we will never know who sent this `"!!!"` into it. The code will work in production, the end users will see no error messages, but somewhere deep inside the program there will be a bug that generates this `"!!!"` instead of `"en"`, or `"fr"`, or some other valid language mnemonic. The bug will sit there unnoticed for many days, months, or even years. Who knows when it will float to the surface and what the damage will be. If it's just one bug, it may not be a big deal. However, if all programmers who work with the software believe in the Fail Safe philosophy, there will many undiscovered bugs that are *protected* by the code around them. This is why Fail Safe is a wrong idea.

The right idea is known as Fail Fast, which means: do not tolerate any incoming arguments or any situations unless you are absolutely happy about them. Do not protect bug makers! Make their mistakes visible as early as possible.

Of course, this means more bugs will be visible to your end-users when you start writing the software. Most of your bugs will be jumping into their faces and your users will complain. Don't let this frustrate you. Software defects are part of the programming process. The more of them you discover, document, and fix, the higher the quality of your software will be. Eventually. If you hide defects and protect their makers, your program will be bug-free when it's young. However, as it starts maturing, the amount of bugs will start growing and it'll be more difficult to fix them. On the contrary, if you make defects obvious and visible as much as possible, you will have many of them at the beginning, when the software is young. However, when it gets bigger and older, the density of bugs will drop and the maintainability will be much higher.

How do we make bugs visible? We throw *exceptions*. For example:

```
greeting: function(n, lang) {
  if (lang.length != 2) {
    throw "The locale is wrong";
  }
  // The rest of the code
}
```

The `throw` statement here is what will cause the execution of the method to stop immediately and create an *exceptional* situation for those who have called it. They will have to deal with the exception somehow. For example:

```
lucy.greeting("Sarah", "!!!");
console.log("Let's start!");
```

The second line will not be executed. The `greeting` will *throw* the `"The locale is wrong"` exception, which will turn a smaller bug into a larger one. The exception will bubble up to the a higher level, and it will go on until someone finally *catches* it and does something.

It's very good practice to throw exceptions here and there to protect yourself against defective code and incorrect inputs. It's also good practice to not throw meaningless exceptions, like we just did: `"The locale is wrong"`. It's important to provide as much detail in the exception message as possible to help someone at the higher level understand what exactly the reason for failure was. For example, this would be a much better *input check*:

```
greeting: function(n, lang) {
  if (lang.length != 2) {
    throw "The locale " + lang +
      " is wrong, exactly two characters expected";
  }
  // The rest of the code
}
```

We build a longer text with more detail, which will help those who make mistakes at the higher level understand what they did wrong. Just saying that "the locale is wrong" is far from enough. This message will most likely confuse the caller and they won't be interested in fixing the bug. They will blame us and suspect that the bug is on our side. To avoid this, we must make our exception messages as verbose and detailed as possible.

Of course, we have to remember that the message may end up on the user screen or a public web page. That's why we shouldn't include any sensitive data in there. For example, this would be totally wrong:

```
if (p !== password)
    throw "The password " + p
        + " doesn't match the expected password "
        + password;
  }
  // The rest of the code
}
```

However this one is more or less OK:

```
    if (p !== password)
        throw "The password " + "*".repeat(p.length)
            + " doesn't match the expected "
            + "*".repeat(password.length);
    }
    // The rest of the code
}
```

It will throw something like this (some security experts may still complain):

```
The password ****** doesn't match the expected ****
```

The bottom line is that we have to throw exceptions often and make them as informative as possible. Later, at some other place of the program, exceptions are caught and dealt with. For example:

```
try {
  // Some large piece of code, where
  // many different problems may occur
  // and exceptions will be thrown
} catch (e) {
   console.log("There is a problem: " + e.message);
}
```

There will be many places in your program where exceptions are thrown. The more frequently you do this, the better. However, there should ideally be only one place where you catch them and do something with them. In this example, we just catch and print the message to the console. In real-life applications, you'll probably somehow show the error to the user, maybe record it somewhere in the file for later dispatching and analysis, and so on.

★

Why may some consider showing `****` in the logs a security threat?

★★

Why do you think I format multi-line string concatenation the way I do it, starting each consecutive line with a `+`?

★★

In which industries, aside from software development, is Fail Fast philosophy applicable?

★★

How would you catch an exception and print its *stacktrace* to the console?

★★

Explain how `finally` works in JavaScript.

★★★

Read *JavaScript: the Definitive Guide (2006)* by Flanagan [5].

Chapter 3

Third

This chapter will not be about writing code, but about making sure it works and doesn't fall apart. Honestly, I believe that this chapter is the most important for you if you want to become a senior software engineer. No matter how junior you are now, eventually you will learn how to code. However, there is a very long journey from a collection of source code files to a software package that can be delivered, used, and sold. Most programmers never reach the destination point and remain code writers instead of becoming software developers. I hope you don't make this mistake.

3.1 Version control

As we agreed before, a program is a collection of text files. Each file has its own name and extension. In order to execute a program, the Runtime puts files together, interprets them, and does what their instructions are telling it do. Each file is *created* and *modified* by you, a programmer. When a group of programmers are working with the same program, they will modify files at the same time. Some of them may work with a group of files, while others are editing other files, but usually programmers want to be able to edit any file they see, when necessary.

You can imagine how chaotic the work of a group of software developers would be if they all sent each other their files over email, starting their messages with something like "Hey Johnny, take a look at this ZIP archive, I've modified `src/main.java` and `src/x/test.java`." With just two developers and a few files, this might not be a problem, but with a team of ten and a large project, it would simply be impossible.

Another problem that you will face once you start writing your first program would be related to your permanent fear of losing the work you've already done. And I'm not talking about losing your laptop at the airport—this may never happen to you. I'm talking about the moment of "Damn, I just deleted the code that worked yesterday, how do I get it back?" It happens to me almost every week.

And there is one more problem that has to be solved by a team of programmers. We may want to know who wrote what and why when we look at the lines of code. Just seeing the instructions, statements, and operators may not be enough to understand what they all mean. We want to know *why* their authors wrote them and when. We need to see the *history* of changes to better understand how the software works and make modifications faster.

To solve these three problems *version control systems* (VCS) were created a long time ago. At the time of writing of this book, Git is the standard de facto tool. You have to use it right from the beginning, and it is as simple as these five steps:

1. Clone a repository from the server;
2. Start a new branch from the trunk (`master` in Git);
3. Modify some files and commit your changes;
4. Merge your branch back to the trunk;
5. Push your local copy to the server.

Step 1. A *repository* is a collection of files together with *all* their previous versions. If your project is old enough, the repository will be huge, even though it may contain just a few files. That's because aside from your text files it contains the information about their authors, dates, and all changes made. This is how any *decentralized* VCS is designed. When you *clone* it, you download the entire database to your laptop, which may take some time and consume a lot of bandwidth. Once you have, you have an identical copy of what the server has. For example, to clone GitHub repository `yegor256/jo` you do:

```
$ git clone https://github.com/yegor256/jo
$ cd jo
```

Step 2. Then, you branch from the *trunk*, automatically creating copies of all of the files and directories, making them ready for modifications. A *branch* is a temporary working copy of your project that you can modify in any way you want without fear of breaking anything in the trunk. You may also work with a number of features at the same time, trying to implement them and failing. Or they may just take time to implement. You don't want those development processes to clash; you want to keep them isolated. To achieve this, you implement each feature in its own branch. Professional developers may have dozens of branches at the same time, switching between them multiple times an hour. You never develop directly in the trunk, you always *branch out* first. Here is how you create a new branch in Git, where `123` is the name of the branch:

```
$ git branch 123
```

Step 3. When you are done with making changes to the files, you *commit* them to the branch, letting VCS know that you are ...done. Each modification you are committing to a branch is a called a *commit*, and it has an author, a date, and a unique *hash*. If you know the hash of the commit, you can always find it in the entire history of the repository. This is how you commit changes to your local Git repository:

```
$ git add .
$ git commit -am 'new ideas implemented'
```

Step 4. Eventually, one of your branches will be good enough to be *merged* to the trunk. By that time, the branch may have many commits, which you've created during a few days of work. When you merge, they all go to the trunk together in a batch. However, you may have *merge conflicts* if some other branch modified the same files you are trying to modify with your current branch. You will have to *resolve* those conflicts, deciding which changes make more sense: yours or those which are in the trunk already. This is how you switch back to the `master` branch in Git and merge your `123` branch into it:

```
$ git checkout master
$ git merge 123
```

Step 5. Finally, you may want to *push* your local copy back to the server to let other programmers *pull* them and see what you've done. Even if you work alone, you should push your changes to the server often to make sure you don't lose everything when your laptop, God forbid, gets stolen at the airport. This is how you push your `master` branch back to GitHub:

```
$ git push origin master
```

You absolutely must understand how Git works, down to the very little details. Without this knowledge, you will always be a junior engineer, constantly asking more senior colleagues to help you.

★
When exactly were the first VCS products created and what were their names?

★
Explain the difference between centralized and decentralized version control systems, and name three pros and cons of each of them.

★
What are the largest open source repositories in the world? Name ten of them. How many files are there, and what is the total size in bytes of each repository?

★
What is the name of the trunk in Git? How about Subversion? Find out what it's named in five other version control systems.

★ ★
Clone the repository of www.takes.org project and count how many commits I've made there.

★★
Explain what *commit messages* are for and what problems may arise in their absence.

★★
Explain what happens in the case of Git hash collision.

★★
Explain what `.gitignore` file is for.

★★
Explain how "squash" commits work.

★★
Explain the *revert* operation in version control.

★★★
Explain what GitFlow is.

★★★
Read *Version Control with Git (2012)* by Loeliger and McCullough [13].

3.2 Pull request

You will never work alone if and when you become a professional software developer. Even if you work alone, you will still have people around you who will be interested in *contributing* to what you're doing because the majority of your code will be *open source* code. I'm sure you've heard these words, but I'll explain anyway.

To create a more or less decent piece of software, you will need to use modules and components created by other programmers, whom you may never know. It's simply impossible nowadays to imagine programmers writing everything from scratch and never using software packages created by others. This was possible to imagine thirty years ago, but not anymore.

I just checked one of my web applications just now. It has over five thousand lines of code. I also checked how many software modules it depends on and uses. There are 23. The total size of them is over 120 thousand lines of code, and I'm not counting Ruby, the programming language, and Linux, the operating system, which my web application is working on. You can compare the numbers. 5K LoC written by myself and 120K LoC written by somebody else I don't know. My contribution is smaller than 5% and I call this web app "mine."

It is fair? How does it work? Those 23 software modules are provided to me by volunteers, who wrote them for free, not even expecting a "Thank you" from me. Actually, they won't mind if I drop them an email, but this isn't what this game is about. Those people are just passioned about software development, and they want to share their results with others. This is a well-known phenomenon of altruism, which has driven the software industry forward for the last thirty years, or more. It seems that it won't ever cease, and we will continue to have more open source software modules and libraries.

One day you may also want to join this army of volunteers, who are actually the elite of our software industry, and create something of your own that everybody else will enjoy using.

The most phenomenal part of the open source phenomenon is that the majority of freely available software products are created by groups of people who barely know each other, if at all. They work online, never seeing each other. If you look at some large and popular open source product, you will see that it has a large group of *contributors*, which includes people who make small changes to different files and then walk away, never returning back. Those changes may be *bug fixes*, small features, or maybe typo corrections. The larger and more popular the product, the bigger the amount of modifications it receives everyday.

Open source volunteers never work alone. The market simply won't let them stay alone. Once they publish their product online and let us it, we will start finding bugs there or some functionality blank spots. We may email them when we want those problems to be fixed, or we may fix them ourselves and send them GitHub *pull requests*. This is how I would do it, if I want to correct a typo in an open source module I'm using in my web app:

Step 1. First, I make a full copy of their repository, which is known as a *fork*. I have to do that because they won't let me push my branch to their repository, mostly for security reasons—they don't know me. My fork is mine and I can do whatever I want with it.

Step 2. Next, in my own fork, I create a new branch where I can fix the typo and make sure I don't break anything. I make the changes and commit them to my branch. Then, I push the branch to my fork, which is on the server, where they can see it. Everything happens in my fork and they don't know anything about it yet.

Step 3. Finally, I ask them to pull, creating a pull request. I *request* them to pull, hence the name. They review my changes and if they like them, they merge my branch into their trunk. Done. I'm an open source contributor and everybody who is using this product will enjoy the code I wrote.

This process is full of excitement and frustrations. When your code gets accepted by a large and well-known product, you will be very happy. A few years ago, I met a pretty rich venture capital investor who told me a story how he managed to make a correction to the Linux core, and got an email from Linus Torvalds. This happened maybe ten years before we met, but he was still proud of that. Indeed, contributing something meaningful to the core of Linux is an achievement. On the other hand, you will be frustrated when your pull request is *rejected* because of low quality of code or some other reasons. It often happens to me, too.

To be a professional programmer, you have to be an open source contributor and an author of open source modules, components, packages, libraries and products. There is no way out of this game. Get used to its rules.

★
Name ten of the most popular open source software products. What do you think made them popular?

★
How many contributors are in Docker, Chromium, Nginx, and Ruby Language? Who of them are the most active?

★ ★ ★
Find out how big the open source market was thirty years ago, comparing it to the size of the proprietary software market. Find the same pair of numbers today. Email them to me and I will send you a free copy of *Elegant Objects* book.

★ ★ ★
Pick one of the largest open source projects. Find a typo in their code or documentation and submit a pull request. Make sure it is accepted and merged.

3.3 Unit test

Take a look at this code one more time:

```
const lucy = {
  greet: function(name, locale) {
    if (locale == "fr") {
      console.log("Bonjour, " + name);
    } else {
      console.log("Hello, " + name);
    }
  }
};
```

We can try how it works:

```
> lucy.greet("Yegor", "en");
Hello, Yegor
```

It works, doesn't it? How do we know? We just executed it and can *visually* confirm that it works. This is good enough as long as we remember what the *expected output* of our method `greet` is. What if we leave this method for a few months and come back to it later, trying to check whether it works or not? Will we remember that the right output is `"Hello, Yegor"` instead of, for example, `"Hey, Yegor"`? What if we give this code to a friend and ask them to improve it? The friend will want to check whether it still works before touching it. If it's already broken and doesn't do what it's supposed to do, it's better to fix it first and then improve, right?

We can, of course, write a short documentation:

```
const lucy = {
  // This method is supposed to print "Hello, Jeff"
  // to the console if you call it like this:
  // lucy.greet("Jeff", "en")
  // However, if you call it with "fr" locale
  // it will print "Bonjour, Jeff".
  greet: function(name, locale) {
    // And here goes the code
  }
};
```

This documentation will help us understand the method in the future, but we will still have to run it to check whether it still works. And software breaks very often. This may surprise you, but something you write today that works may not work tomorrow, and you won't understand why. This documentation block is a great message to the future self, if that future self is interested in reading it.

Even if you will be interested in doing what the documentation block says, you may fail to do it simply because it'll be too difficult. This simple method is not a good example, because ...it's really simple. It won't be a problem to run it in a year and see what it prints. In bigger examples, this will not be the case. Larger and more complex methods will not be that easy to run; they will need some preparation beforehand. And the results they will return will need much more detailed validation than just a visual check of whether `"Bonjour, Jeff"` is there or not.

To solve this problem of the code that is written today and must be *automatically* validated tomorrow, unit tests were invented. Here is how such a test would look:

```
lucy.greet("Louise", "fr");
const printed = // Grab the text just printed
if ("Bonjour, Louise" !== printed) {
   throw "lucy.greet() printed this: " + printed;
}
```

First, we ask `lucy` to say hello to Louise. Then, we catch the output produced (we will discuss this step in a minute). Finally, we compare the expected output with the actual one. If they don't match, we throw an exception. The code we just wrote is called an *automated test* because it tests the object `lucy` automatically, without our participation. All we need to do is just run it and see what it says. If it doesn't say anything, our code inside the object `lucy` is still OK. However, if it throws an exception, something is wrong.

Professional programmers actively use automated tests as a tool to support their code writing activities. Here is how: when they start working with a new *feature* or a *bug fix*, they run the entire *test suite* to check whether all tests are still *green* (a test is "green" if it doesn't throw any exceptions; a test is "red" if it raises a signal about something that is broken). If one of them is red, they don't start working with the code base. Programmers fix the code to make the test green again.

Then, when all tests are green, the programmer makes the changes they want to make. When the changes are ready, the programmer runs all of the tests again. If all of them are green, the programmer is happy and commits the code to the repository. Then, a good programmer, adds a few *new* tests to *cover* the functionality just added or modified. Finally, all of the tests are run together again and the job is done. Without a big enough and well-designed test suite, it would be difficult to modify any part of the code base without being scared of breaking something.

★
What is *Fear Driven Development*?

★
What is *Test Driven Development*? What is the main principle of it?

★★
What is the difference between *debugging* and unit testing?

★★
What is the difference between *integration* and unit tests?

★★
Explain what *test code coverage* is.

★★
What is the difference between raising an exception and using `assert` in Java?

★★
Read *Test-Driven Development (2003)* by Beck [1].

★★★
Name and explain five qualities of a good unit test.

★★★
Name five unit-testing *anti-patterns* and explain what's wrong with them.

★★★
Read *The Art of Software Testing (2011)* by Myers, Sandler, and Badgett [16].

3.4 Mock

Here is how we tested `lucy` a few pages ago:

```
lucy.greet("Louise", "fr");
const printed = // Grab the text just printed
if ("Bonjour, Louise" !== printed) {
  throw "lucy.greet() printed this: " + printed;
}
```

However, it wasn't explained how exactly we "grab the text just printed." How can we catch what `greet` is sending to the console in order to verify that it's the message we need? The method `greet` of the object `lucy` just calls method `log` of the object `console`, and it does the job. We need to find a way to *intercept* the call and save the message being sent to the `printed` variable. Luckily, JavaScript makes it possible:

```
const printed = '';
const before = console.log;
console.log = function(text) {
  printed = text;
}
lucy.greet("Louise", "fr");
console.log = before;
```

First, we get the method `log` from the object `console` and assign it to the variable `before`. In JavaScript, every method is an object too (also known as *function*), which you can manipulate the same way you manage any other objects. Then, we assign a different function to the attribute `log` of the object `console`. This function is not printing anything to the console, but rather it saves whatever is coming in into the variable `printed`. Then, we ask `lucy` to do the job in the method `greet`. It will ask the `console` to `log()`, not knowing that it's not the original method, but a *fake* version of it. Finally, we put back the original method to let all other tests to use the console in the way it's intended to be used.

This process is known as *mocking*, and the function that replaced the original `log` is known as the *mock object* (or the mock method).

This way of mocking is terrible practice. However, this is the only way to test `lucy` because `lucy` is *not test-friendly*. It is hard-wired to the object `console` and this dependency is *unbreakable*. The object `lucy` depends on the object `console` because it uses its method `log`. This is normal. Objects depend on each other, they can't work in isolation. However, making them *tightly coupled* is a bad idea; `lucy` will always work with `console` and nobody can change that. This is what tight coupling means in this case.

The solution is to turn `console` into an *injectable* dependency:

```
const lucy = {
  greet: function(name, locale, c = console) {
    if (locale == "fr") {
      c.log("Bonjour, " + name);
    } else {
      c.log("Hello, " + name);
    }
  }
};
```

Now, the method `greet` has an additional third argument `c`, which is supposed to be an object that has a method `log`. If `c` is not provided, it will refer to the object `console`, which is defined by the JavaScript runtime. Now we can ask `lucy` to say "hello" in two different ways:

```
lucy.greet("Louise", "fr");
lucy.greet("Louise", "fr", fake);
```

The first call will substitute `c` with `console` and the message will show up on the screen. The second call will give it the object `fake`, which has to be defined beforehand. The unit test may look like this, if `console` is an injectable dependency:

```
const fake = {
  printed: "",
  log: function(text) {
    this.printed = text;
  }
};
lucy.greet("Louise", "fr", fake);
if ("Bonjour, Louise" !== fake.printed) {
  throw "lucy.greet() printed this: " + fake.printed;
}
```

The beauty of this approach is that it's *side-effect free*. In order to test `lucy`, we don't need to modify anything that is not directly and visually related to it. We don't need to investigate its code first before mocking things around it right. We just read the signature of the method `greet`, and realize that the console is replaceable.

Professional programmers always try to design their objects tests-friendly by making all of its dependencies injectable. Moreover, the best programmers create fake objects together with real ones, in order to simplify testing. In the example above I had to create the `fake` object in order to test `lucy`, but it would be convenient to have it ready, created by those who created the object `console`.

★★
Why is mocking a terrible practice? Find and give three reasons.

★★
What do the terms *coupling* and *cohesion* mean in object-oriented programming? Explain.

★★
Explain the difference between a mock object and a *stub*.

★★
What is *Dependency Injection Container* and how does it work?

★★★
How would you test `lucy` in Java, where it's impossible to replace the method `log` of the object `console`?

3.5 Framework

Take a look at these lines once again:

```
if ("Bon jour, Louise" !== fake.printed) {
   throw "lucy.greet() printed this: " + fake.printed;
}
```

They compare the actual value of `fake.printed` with the expected one, `"Bon jour, Louise"`, and raise an exception if they are not equal. This operation is very common for almost all *test cases*; we always want to compare what actually happened with what we expected to happen. Node.js helps us minimize the amount of lines of code we need write to compare these two values. Here is how:

```
const a = require('assert');
a.strictEqual("Bon jour, Louise", fake.printed);
```

The first line instructs Node.js to *load* a JavaScript file `assert.js`, created by someone else and located somewhere inside Node.js, and then assign what this file *provides* to the constant `a`: an object with methods, like `strictEqual()` and many others. The `assert.js` is part of the Node.js open source *framework*, which is given to us programmers for free, to reduce the time we spend on creating our code.

There are many frameworks in JavaScript world. One of them is Mocha, designed to help us write pretty unit tests. This is how our test would look if we would use Mocha:

```
const mocha = require('mocha');
const a = require('assert');
mocha.describe('lucy', function() {
  mocha.it('mocks the console for logging', function() {
    const fake = {
      printed: "",
      log: function(text) {
        this.printed = text;
      }
    };
    lucy.greet("Louise", "fr", fake);
    a.strictEqual("Bon jour, Louise", fake.printed);
  });
});
```

Methods `describe` and `it` are provided by the object `mocha` *imported* from `mocha.js`. Any programmer who knows JavaScript and Mocha will immediately understand this code and will know exactly what `strictEqual()` is doing.

Frameworks save a lot of time, at the same time enlarging the *learning curve*. Just like any programming language, we have to learn how to use a framework, and it may take some time. However, when it's learned, the speed of development increases.

Sometimes, those frameworks, which introduce many primitive constructs like `strictEqual`, are Domain Specific Languages (DSL). Indeed, after typing `strictEqual` a hundred times you will forget that it's a method of an object loaded from the file `assert`, but will start *feeling* that it's part of the JavaScript language itself. Some programmers get used to these DSLs sometimes so much that they can't write anything in JavaScript, when they land into a project, which is not using the frameworks they are accustomed to. Good examples are Spring for Java and RoR for Ruby: they are so actively used at the moment that most junior programmers when they start learning, for example, Ruby, believe that the features provided by RoR are the features of the Ruby language itself.

This is why, right after picking the programming language, you have to pick the set of frameworks you will be using. For example, when I started to write this book I had to choose which JavaScript unit testing framework to choose. Mocha was one of eight (!) rather popular other frameworks I found on the market. I don't give you their names here because I'm sure that by the time you get this book in your hands the list will look differently. Frameworks change much more frequently than programming languages. Java and Ruby are over 20 years old each, while Spring and RoR are much younger. We had many other frameworks in the Java world before. Most of them are almost dead now.

Does this volatility of the market make us follow all the trends and switch frameworks every time a new one gets popular? Yes, it does. Or maybe it doesn't. Depends on your career strategy and the business strategy of your projects. Staying tightly coupled with a single set of frameworks will definitely make you a professional, who knows every single feature of each of them and can apply them easily. However, you will miss the features and paradigms introduced by more modern frameworks. I would recommend revising your *tech stack* every time you start a new project. Changing horses in a running project is almost always a terrible idea, but while the project is not yet started, there is an opportunity to pick something more interesting and fresh from the market.

There are also *libraries*, which are also collections of tools to make our life simpler, but they are usually smaller than frameworks. There is no hard line between them, but libraries are older and frameworks usually put more constraints on you. Libraries started to exist long time ago, when programmers realized that re-writing the same functionality over and over again from scratch in each project was a bad idea. For example, in one project you need functionality to sort elements in an array. You implement it, test it, deploy it, and it works. Then, in a few months you start a different project and you need to sort an array again. You don't want to implement and test the sorting algorithm once again. You want to *copy* what was done before. Copy and *paste*! However, after you simply copy the files from the first project, you realize that the same source code is now in two places. If you find a bug in it, you will have to fix it twice: in both projects. With two projects this may not be a big problem, but when the amount of projects that need an array to be sorted starts to grow, it becomes very difficult or impossible to *propagate* changes to all copies.

To solve this problem libraries where introduced. You write the array sorting functionality once and package it as a standalone software module. Then, you make both of your projects *dependent* on that library. Every time each project is built, it will *use* the library (or *re-use*). The source code of the array sorting algorithm will stay in one place only. Once we want to modify it, we make the necessary changes and *release* a new *version* of the library.

★
Name five methods, aside from `strictEqual()`, from the object `a` loaded above from the Mocha framework.

★
How many methods are in the `a` object?

★ ★
Run the example above and make sure the test passes.

★ ★
Find three other frameworks that optimize unit testing, similar to Mocha, and explain their pros and cons.

★ ★
What does `const` mean and how is it different from `var`? What is `let`, by the way?

★ ★
Find and list five popular DSLs.

★ ★
What exactly is `require()` and where is it implemented?

★ ★ ★
Name three features of RoR, which Ruby programmers mistakenly attribute to the Ruby language itself.

★ ★ ★
What is the difference between static and shared libraries?

3.6 Package

The `assert.js` file is provided by Node.js itself, while `mocha.js` is not. You have to download it first and place somewhere in your project directory. There will be a few other files that will come together with `mocha.js`. You will need all of them to make Mocha work. At the time of writing, there are 72 files inside the Mocha framework. The entire *package* has to be downloaded and placed where Node.js can find it.

Downloading Mocha and placing its files where Node.js can find them is not very pleasant work. It's very easy to make a mistake or forget something, and it's very time consuming. Moreover, you don't want to commit Mocha files to your Git repository because ...it's a very bad practice. Sooner or later Mocha authors will *release* a new *version* and you will have to do this work again: downloading, unpacking, putting them to the right place, and making sure they work together with your code. Actually, this is what we were doing twenty years ago and it was a very messy process. Luckily, we don't do this anymore because we have *package managers*.

Node.js Package Manager (Npm) is one of them, mostly used for JavaScript projects. We configure it by creating a `package.json` file in the project root directory:

```
{
  "name": "jo",
  "version": "1.0.0",
  "author": "Yegor Bugayenko",
  "license": "MIT",
  "repository": "yegor256/jo",
  "devDependencies": {
    "mocha": "6.1.4"
  }
}
```

This file, as you can probably understand, is an instruction set. The Npm will understand it and do the job when we ask it to at the command line (I recommend you install `npm` using Homebrew):

```
$ npm install
```

It will download Mocha *dependency* (this is how Npm calls packages) and place it in the directory `node_modules`. The number `6.1.4` is the version of Mocha, which is not just a simple number, but a combination of three of them. This method of *labeling* software packages is known as *semantic versioning*.

It's good practice to make your project depend on specific versions of libraries and frameworks, just like we did here with Mocha. It was possible to ignore the version number to specify something like `6.*`, which would mean that we are good to go with any version of Mocha as long as it starts with `6`. However, this may cause problems in the future, like when the author of the library changes the code, introducing or removing some features, and a new version simply won't work with our code.

When the version is changed and we want to use a new one, we just modify the file `package.json`, set a higher version, and run `npm install` once again. Npm will do the work for us, finding the package with the new version at `https://npmjs.com` (this is where most open source JavaScript packages are stored), downloading it, unpacking, and placing into `node_modules`.

★
Explain what these software version labels mean: `0.0.1-ALPHA`, `1.0.19`, `7.9.19-release`.

★ ★
Which version was released earlier: `1.0.13` or `2.0.0-ALPHA`?

★ ★
How many dependencies Mocha has?

★ ★
How exactly does Npm expect us to specify the version of a dependency if we want it to mean "anything that is above `6.0.0`"?

★ ★
Explain when and why *dependency hell* may occur.

★ ★
What is the file `package-lock.json`, which is created by `npm`, for?

★ ★
Name five package managers, besides Npm, and explain the differences between them.

★ ★
What is the difference between `dependencies` and `devDependencies` in the `package.json` configuration?

★ ★ ★
Create and release your own Npm package to `npmjs.org`.

3.7 Build

We already have a few *semantically* separate pieces of code in our small project about Lucy and other "people." One of them is about `lucy`, another one is about `doorman`, yet another one is about testing `lucy`, and so on. Any software project consists of many *pieces* that may do different things. Some of them will be source code files, others will be plain text files, or maybe even images or documentation. A large project may have thousands of files, even though it's discouraged to have too many files in a single repository.

Some projects may do it differently, but it's good practice to place each block of code in its own file. For example, we may have this repository *structure*:

```
README.md
LICENSE.txt
package.json
src/
  lucy.js
  doorman.js
  entrance.js
  vault.js
test/
  test_lucy.js
```

There are two directories—`src` (sources) and `test`—and a single file called `LICENSE.txt`, where we write some standard text explaining how our source code is *allowed* to be used. We may also put a disclaimer there saying something along the lines of: "We are NOT responsible for any damages our software may cause, no matter how and why you decide to use it." Any piece of software should have such a file with the license. You don't need to write it up from scratch, though. There are a few popular licenses that you can just reuse, like MIT, for example.

Now, imagine someone who doesn't know anything about our project opens up this repository and looks at the directory structure and the license file. Will they understand what to do with it, what it's for, and how to run the tests to make sure `lucy` works? They may guess that since there is a `test/test_lucy.js` file, it may test a corresponding file `src/lucy.js`. However, this is only obvious for a small project. When the project gets larger, interconnections and dependencies between files become more complicated and, simply put, messy. Nobody wants to remember what to run to test what. We want to *automate* it all.

Formally speaking, we want to automate the *build*. We want a tool that will build everything for us. A tool that will take all necessary files, run all necessary tests, perform all the necessary checks and manipulations, and create a single file, which is the product to ship to the end-user. If it is a mobile app, we want the `.apk` (Android) or the `.ipa` (iOS) file; if it's a web app in Java, we want the `.war` file; if it is a web site in HTML/JavaScript, we want a directory with files to be *deployed* to the web server, and so on. We want to turn a collection of source code files into a *deployable* binary/text package.

The first most powerful, complex tool for build automation is GNU Make, which expects us to create a plain `Makefile` text file at the first level of the repository to explain the specific order we want to run our tests and what the expected *target* to build is. There are many other build automation tools on the market that are simpler and specifically designed for certain programming languages, like Maven for Java, Rake for Ruby, or Composer for

PHP.

There is also
Grunt for JavaScript, which we will use now. First,
we add it as a dependency to the `package.json`:

```
{
  [...]
  "devDependencies": {
    [...]
    "grunt": "1.0.4",
    "grunt-mocha-test": "0.13.3",
  }
}
```

Next, we ask Npm, the package manager, to find and download
`grunt` and `grunt-mocha-test`. These are two newly added
dependencies:

```
$ npm install
```

Next, we create a configuration file `Gruntfile.js` for Grunt, to
tell it how our application has to be *built*:

```
module.exports = function(grunt) {
  grunt.initConfig({
    pkg: grunt.file.readJSON('package.json'),
    mochaTest: {
      test: {
        src: ['test/**/*.js']
      }
    }
  });
  grunt.loadNpmTasks('grunt-mocha-test');
  grunt.registerTask('default', ['mochaTest']);
};
```

Finally, we start Grunt like this:

```
$ grunt
```

Grunt, like almost all other build tools, understands a project as a collection of *tasks*. To complete the build, all required tasks have to be completed. In this example, we only have one task, which is supposed to use Mocha to run all tests found in the `test` directory. Larger projects may have many more tasks in their builds, sometimes a few dozen. Tests have to be executed; some files have to be archived; some HTML or CSS documents have to be minified; some integration tests have to be executed; and many more. The job of a build tool is to run them one by one, and fail the build if any problems are found, reporting the progress accordingly.

Build automation greatly helps programmers spot problems earlier. In large projects, even a minor modification to a small file may cause problems in other files because they depend on the file you modify. And you don't want to go through all of the tests and run them one by one. You simply won't do it if the build is not automated. You will not run all of the tests or know whether your modifications break anything or not. In the end, everything will be broken. That's why professional programmers start a project with build automation. Before writing any code, they make sure there is a one-liner, like `grunt`, that runs *all* of the tests and raises a red flag when any one of them is broken.

The stronger the build, the better. We want the build to catch all possible mistakes when they show up. In other words, we can say that we want it to be as *fragile* as possible: it should break due to even a minor mistake made.

Ideally, each programmer in a project should run the build before submitting a pull request to the repository to make sure it's still green. However, some programmers may forget and their broken code will get into the repo. If this happens frequently, other programmers may lose *confidence* that the repository contains code that works, and will stop using unit tests as a *safety net* for testing. To prevent this from happening, professional software teams configure their *build pipeline* to prevent any code from getting into the repo before it passes the automated build by running automated *pre-flight* builds.

Say you're a programmer in a team of ten. You start working with a feature, and you make changes in a number of files. Then, you forget to run the build and catch the issues you just caused for some other places in the code. Further, you submit a pull request, and a pre-configured server starts running the build and checks how it's doing. Obviously, it fails and the server rejects the pull request, asking you to fix the issues. It happens over and over again until the code in your branch is good enough to pass the automated build. Eventually, your code gets into the trunk and doesn't break it.

Some teams configure their server to run the build every night and after each modification is pushed to the trunk, just to check that nothing is broken. This process is called *continuous integration*.

★ ★
Explain the pros and cons of using JSON instead of XML as a configuration file.

★ ★
Find 10 large open source JavaScript projects. Calculate how many `.js` files they have and how many lines of code there are in total.

★★
Why is it discouraged to have too many files in a single repository? Some software experts and companies may believe otherwise. Why?

★★
Explain the difference between npm scripts and `Gruntfile` tasks used above.

★★
Name five of the most popular open source licenses and explain the difference between them.

★★
Create a `Makefile` for our repository, and configure it to run all tests from the `test` directory and fail if at least one of them fails.

★★
Try to explain the difference between continuous integration and continuous delivery.

3.8 Static analysis

Good code is code anyone can easily read and understand. Even though this may sound obvious, it was not the case twenty years ago. When computers were slow and expensive, good code was small and worked fast. I remember a competition we had when I was a student: who can write the same algorithm using the least commands, lines of code, and memory. Large programs were slow, and therefore unusable. Sometimes, it was impossible to even run a program on certain computers if there was not enough memory for it.

Those times are almost over. The hardware is getting less

expensive, while programmers are demanding larger compensation, every year. You may want to read my article *We are Done with "Hacking"* published in the Communications of the ACM, Volume 61, Number 7. Long story short, your code should be written mostly for your friends, not just for your computer. Your code should be maintainable, as we discussed earlier in Section 1.9. However, it's much easier said than done. Not all of us understand readability like everybody else. Say you think that this code is readable:

```
door.enter(
  [
    "Jeff",
    "Judy",
    "Sarah"
  ]
);
```

While I believe that it has to be written like this:

```
door.enter(["Jeff", "Judy", "Sarah"]);
```

Even though both your code and my code work just fine, they look very different. I will not like yours because it takes so many lines and is difficult for me to read. You, on the other hand, will not like mine since it's too tight and difficult to modify by adding a new element to the array. The problem is that we will never find a compromise. You will always have a point. I will too.

If you only write for yourself, you may use your own *coding style*, no matter how unusual it is, whether I like it or not. However, if you work in a team, it's important to use the same style that every other team member does. This is how maintainability can be achieved—by deciding what the style is for all of us and enforcing it.

It's not enough to just agree how we write the code. We must make sure nobody violates our agreement. *Static analysis* is what professional programmers use to achieve this. A special software reads our *source files* and points us to the places that should be improved in order to make the code compliant with our coding style. Usually, *static analyzers*, also known as *linters*, are designed to verify one programming language. For example, Checkstyle verifies Java code, Rubocop checks Ruby code, cpplint finds errors in C++ sources, and so on.

Good programmers listen to what static analyzers tell them. They learn from what they recommend and improve their code. Let's apply ESLint, a static analyzer for JavaScript code, to our code base, and see what it says. We just need to add this line to the `package.json` file first:

```
{
  [...]
  "devDependencies": {
    [...]
    "eslint": "5.15.3",
    "grunt-eslint": "21.0.0",
    "eslint-config-google": "0.12.0"
  }
}
```

Then, we add these few lines to the `Gruntfile.js` file:

```
module.exports = function(grunt) {
  grunt.initConfig({
    [...]
    eslint: {
      options: {
        configFile: '.eslintrc.json'
      },
      target: ['src/**/*.js', 'test/**/*.js']
    }
  });
  grunt.loadNpmTasks('grunt-eslint');
  grunt.registerTask('default', ['mochaTest', 'eslint']);
};
```

Finally, we create a configuration file `.eslintrc.json` to explain to ESLint what coding style we would like to adhere to (which is `google`):

```
{
  "env": {
    "es6": true
  },
  "extends": "google"
}
```

Now, we are ready to check our code base and see what problems we have:

$ grunt

29 problems were found. This is how "ugly" my code is now. Functionality wise it's OK. The unit tests are passing, but the coding style is not as good as Google developers would expect from me. I have to fix all of the complaints and make a new commit. I will do that right now.

★ ★
Name ten of the most interesting ESLint checks, as you see them.

★ ★
What do you think I meant above by saying that the algorithm was "occupying less memory"?

3.9 Test coverage

When the package management is configured, the build is automated, unit tests are created, and the static analyzer doesn't complain, good programmers add one more element to the picture to call the project ready for active development: test coverage analysis.

When Mocha runs the `test_lucy.js` test, it calls certain methods of certain objects from the `src` directory. How many of them are being called during the entire test run? How many of them did we miss? The more we call, the better our test suite. The more we miss, the weaker our testing. The exact number can be given by a test coverage analysis, which can be done by Istanbul toolkit. We add it as a dependency to the `package.json`:

```
{
  [...]
  "devDependencies": {
    [...]
    "istanbul": "0.4.5",
    "grunt-mocha-istanbul": "5.0.2",
  }
}
```

And configure a new task in the `Gruntfile.js`:

```
module.exports = function(grunt) {
  grunt.initConfig({
    [...]
    mocha_istanbul: {
      coverage: {
        src: 'test',
        options: {
          'timeout': 20000,
          'report-formats': 'html',
          'print': 'summary',
          'check': {
            lines: 60,
            statements: 70,
            functions: 100,
            branches: 50
          }
        }
      }
    }
  });
  grunt.loadNpmTasks('grunt-mocha-istanbul');
  grunt.registerTask(
    'default', ['mocha_istanbul', 'eslint']
  );
};
```

Now, when we run the usual `grunt`, a coverage report is generated in the `coverage` directory. It's in HTML format, so you can open it with Safari. It shows which lines of code were *covered* by the tests.

Istanbul also fails the build if the coverage metrics are below the required threshold, configured in the `Gruntfile.js` file, which includes four numbers: lines coverage, statements coverage, functions coverage, and branch coverage. The higher the numbers, the stronger the testing of the code, and the higher the quality of the product. However, some experts argue with this claim and I understand them. Indeed, it's not that simple and software with a very high coverage, close to 100%, may still have a lot of functionality defects. But software with a very low coverage is definitely not something you should be proud of.

★ ★
What is the difference between path coverage and statement coverage?

★ ★
Explain the idea of *mutation coverage*.

★ ★ ★
Calculate the test coverage of the Mocha framework itself.

3.10 DevOps

There is one last thing to do before we can call our software product a product: We *release* it so that everybody can see it on the Internet. In order to do that, we need to *package* it and *deploy*. In each programming language and type of software, the process is different, but these two ultimate goals are always present. First, we put all existing artifacts together. Artifacts such as source code files, documentation files, maybe some plain text documents, images, maybe video or sound files (if we are creating a game), and create a *package* ready to be delivered to end-users. Second, we send this package to some place where users can find it.

For example, every time Mocha developers create a new version, they package their 72 files and send them to npmjs.org. This is where all other JavaScript developers find them. Each new version release means packaging and deploying. Good programmers know that no matter how good they are, they make mistakes. That's why before releasing a new version, they build it, which means executing all tests, statically analyzing the source code, and checking the test coverage. If everything looks good and the build is green, they package and deploy.

Thus, the build pipeline we discussed before becomes longer and turns into a *release pipeline*, involving more components that are usually outside of our, the programmers', control. Usually, the server we deploy to is managed by people known as *web admins* or even large departments of them known as *operations* groups. They are not responsible for developing new software, but rather for making sure the software already created operates the way it should.

Some time ago, it became obvious that keeping developers isolated from operations was not a good idea. Developers want to know how their software operates, and operation guys are interested to know how we develop it. Moreover, good developers want to design the software with the specifics of the operations environment it will be running in. Say we create our JavaScript software using some features of the 9th edition of ECMAScript.

However, after the deployment, it doesn't work. We blame the operations since everything worked just fine on our laptops, but they tell us that the deployment *environment* only supports the 6th version of ECMAScript. Whose fault is it? Who's to blame?

Both. We didn't ask them upfront what the supported ECMAScript version was on *production* servers, and they didn't share this information with us, also upfront. To avoid such miscommunication issues and to put developers and operations closer to each other, some time ago we started to melt these two roles and introduced a new one called *DevOps*. These new people are neither programmers, nor operations—they are both. They know how to write code, package, deploy, and how to make sure it runs without errors in production.

Actually, DevOps is more of a skill than a role. Good programmers must understand all of this and may not only focus on coding anymore. If you don't know how to package your software and understand how it works on the server, you are limiting yourself and only doing your career a disservice.

★
Who exactly introduced the DevOps term first and when?

★
Explain what ECMAScript is.

★★
Read *Continuous Delivery (2010)* by Humble and Farley [11].

★★
What other environments may exist, aside of production? What is the difference between them?

★ ★
Explain what containerization is.

3.11 Lifecycle

As you can see, writing code is not the only thing that needs to be done in order to create a working software product. There have to be tests, builds, package managing, release pipelines, and many more. Yes, this is not the entire picture. The full picture is bigger and its formal name is *Software Development Life Cycle* (SDLC). I can't give you a full summary of everything it includes because in larger projects, there could be things we can't even predict in this book, but mid-size projects are all the same. Their lifecycles must include the same elements. Some or most projects omit certain elements, like not writing unit tests or not checking their code bases with static analyzers, but it's only their fault. The lifecycle of an ideal, mid-size software project must look like the following flow of activities (bold text indicates the expected deliverables):

Plans. First, we sit together and *estimate* how the project can be completed. We plan many things, but the most important five are: *time, cost, scope, quality,* and *risks*. Even though the famous Triple Constraint includes only three (time, cost, and scope), many experts think this is not enough: we must also plan the quality we expect to achieve, and the risks we are going to mitigate or accept. We also have to identify our *stakeholders*—who do we develop the software for.

Requirements. Then, we *solicit* and *analyze* requirements. We document, enumerate, prioritize, and *validate* them. We make sure all stakeholders understand and agree with them, which is the most difficult part of requirements management.

Architecture. Then, we decide what the pieces our software product should be made of; how they should connect and communicate; how we will test them; and what the design of our release pipeline will be. We explain our ideas using Unified Modeling Language (UML).

Code and Unit Tests. Then, we *implement* the decisions made in the architecture by writing the source code together with unit tests. We commit and push our changes to VCS *feature* branches, which we then turn into *merge requests*.

Code Reviews. Next, we ask somebody else (a fellow programmer) to review our code. Each review usually means some corrections and criticism, which we have to address in order to get an *approval* for the merge request.

Merges. When code reviewers confirm that a merge request looks good, we attempt to merge the changes after running the build again to be sure that new modifications don't break it.

Releases. Next, we package and deploy the product to the environment where testers and/or end-users can see it.

Bugs. Next, we ask *functional testers* to take a look at the product and report bugs. The more they report, the better, because this is how we increase the quality of software: the more bugs we find, the less our end-users will.

Finally, we start over. We go through this cycle over and over again, as frequently as possible, *incrementally* evolving the software. A properly functioning software team must produce a few new versions of the software each week. A perfectly functioning one can do it a few times a day. A lousy one may tell you that too many releases compromise stability and should be avoided. That's why they only release once a month and it takes a full working day, usually on weekends, and everybody gets stressed. Don't buy this; they just don't know what they're doing.

Actually, many years ago, most software teams believed that the right way to develop software is similar to how we build houses: we plan everything upfront; we purchase the materials; we build the basement, walls, roof, then everything else; and finally we call the customer and show them the house they can live in. This approach was called Waterfall and worked just fine when projects were large, well-funded, and nobody really cared about their success.

However, it became obvious that building software systems and building houses are two fundamentally different processes. The software is much softer. It can be built faster, easier, and with much more flexibility. No need to wait until the roof is complete. It's possible to demonstrate something half-done to customers, get their feedback, and modify requirements until it's too late. Rational Unified Process (RUP) was one of the alternatives to Waterfall, which suggested organizing the lifecycle *iteratively* and not waiting until everything was ready. There were many other methodologies after RUP, but most of them are based on the same principle: deliver as frequently as possible. You don't need to know their names and details, just remember the steps listed above and the key principle; that is enough.

★

Explain who a stakeholder is and name five examples.

★★

What is eXtreme Programming (XP), and what are its pros and cons?

★★

Explain how MoSCoW method works.

★★

Explain the difference between validation and verification.

★★

What is the difference between a feature branch and a `master` branch in Git?

★★

What is the difference between merge requests mentioned here and pull requests mentioned in the Section 3.1?

★★★

What else is in the SWEBOK that I missed in the description of the SDLC above?

★★★

What are the key differences between Microsoft Solutions Framework (MSF) and Rational Unified Process (RUP)?

★★

Read *Peer Reviews in Software (2002)* by Wiegers [19].

★★★

Read *PMP exam prep (2009)* by Rita Mulcahy et al. [17].

Chapter 4

Fourth

Enough of abstract discussions, it's time to get our hands dirty and create something meaningful. In this final chapter we will write a program, which is a game known as Space Invaders. The first version was designed in 1978 by Tomohiro Nishikado for the Atari computer, which was executing ... how many instructions per second, do you think? Just 1.2 million (compare that to the billions our laptops demonstrate now). And it was a very impressive speed at that time. I won't explain the game to you. Find it on the Internet and play a little bit. We will create something similar, but not exactly the same. In our game, there will be invaders, a laser, and a bullet flying straight up in order to destroy the invaders.

We will create the game in a few iterations. In each iteration, we will try to perform all lifecycle steps explained in the previous chapter to illustrate the process.

Let me interrupt you and remind that the code you see in this book can be found in `yegor256/jo` GitHub repository. Clone it to your laptop (more about it in the Section 3.1):

```
$ git clone https://github.com/yegor256/jo
$ cd jo
```

Then, list all the tags available:

```
$ git tag
```

You will see the list of tags related to the sections in the book. Pick one of them and check it out, for example:

```
$ git checkout 3.mock
```

If you find any bugs there, don't hesitate to submit an issue or, even better, a pull request.

4.1 Requirements

As good software engineers always do, let's start creating our software game from defining the requirements. The key element of a requirements document is the *glossary*, which in our case, may look like this:

```
"Laser" is a horizontally moving bar
   at the bottom of the screen.
"Invader" is a horizontally moving bar at the top
   of the screen, lowering the position every time
   it hits the border of the screen.
"Bullet" is a small circle moving from the bottom
   to the top of the screen in an attempt
   to destroy an Invader.
"User" is a human with a web browser.
```

A glossary helps everybody in the project understand key terms and use the same language to communicate. The majority of problems with understanding requirements happen because software teams don't have glossaries of their projects. I'm sure that the project you are working in right now, or will be working when you start programming for money, doesn't have a glossary. Very few of them do, which is very sad. A glossary must be visible to everybody in the team and must be regularly updated, when a new term "joins" the project.

Of course, the glossary may/should not define all terms used in the project. For example, our glossary doesn't specify what a "browser" or a "screen" are. These things are common for most software projects, so we don't describe them in our glossary. But I decided to describe the `User` because in different software products it could mean different things; a mobile app user is not the same as a user of a web site, and so on.

All glossary terms will be capitalized in the text below. I'm suggesting you do the same in your requirements documentation to emphasize the fact that you are talking about our "Bullet" instead of some generic bullet.

Now, when the glossary is ready, we have to define *product statement*, which is a short one sentence answering these five questions: 1) Who is the customer? 2) What do they want? 3) What is the market offering now? 4) What is wrong with existing offers? 5) How will our product fix this? For our simple web-base game, the statement may sound like this:

```
It is a simple JavaScript web game designed
to explain most important concepts of object-oriented
programming and illustrate the book 'Junior Objects'
with practical examples.
```

Even though this text doesn't answer the questions explicitly, it addresses every one of them. Who are the customers? Obviously, the readers of the "Junior Objects" book. What do they want? To learn the most important concepts of OOP. What is the market offering now and what is wrong with existing offers? Nothing, since there is no game to illustrate the book yet. How will our product fix this? We will have a game that illustrates the book.

Now, let's specify the *requirements*, as we understand them now:

```
R1: The User can move the Laser left and right
    with arrow keys.
R2: The User can fire Bullets by pressing
    the Space key.
R3: The System can place Invaders on the screen,
    increasing their amount and the speed
    of movement.
R4: The User can destroy an Invader by hitting it
    with a flying Bullet.
R5: The System can stop the game and show the score
    when any Invader touches the Laser.
```

You probably noticed that all of the requirements are specified in the same format: "somebody `can` do something." Here, "somebody" could be one of the *actors*, like the `User` or the `System`, and each requirement is a simplified form of a *use case*.

There are only two actors in our small game, but in larger applications there will be more and they should be listed as well before we start specifying requirements. If we picture our system as a black box, all of its actors will stay outside of the box and all their use cases will be located inside the box, like at this Use Case UML diagram (the *System under Development* (SuD) is also the actor):

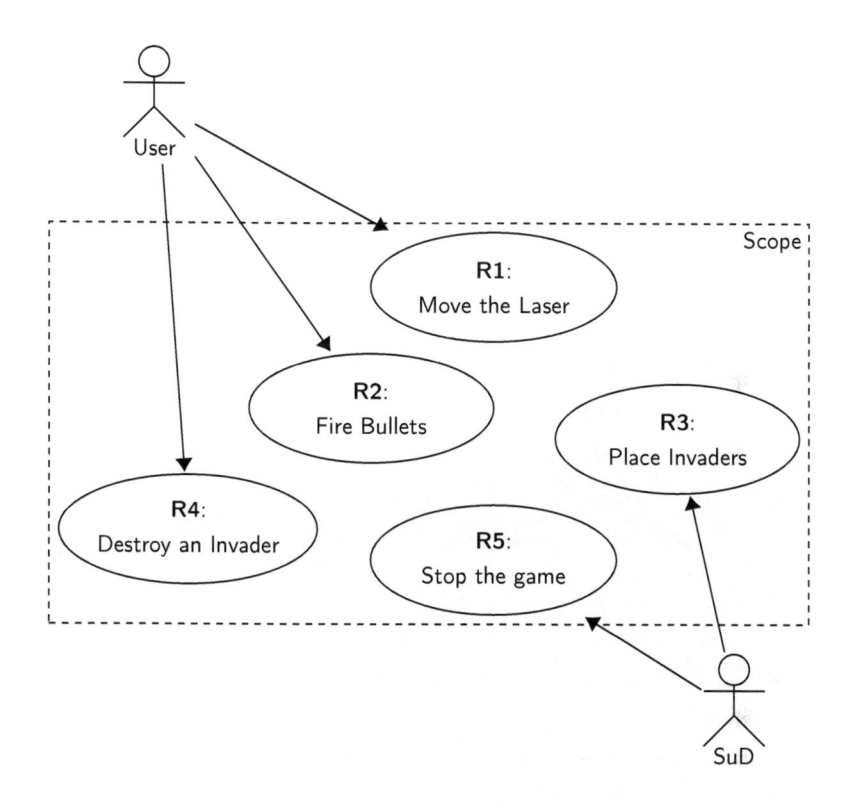

Figure 4.1: UML Use Case Diagram of Space Invaders

The entire set of all use cases constitute the *scope* of the system. If and when all of them are implemented and accepted by the customer, the project is finished; the scope is complete. You probably won't draw this diagram in your projects while they are small. Later, when they grow bigger, without diagrams your product will quickly turn into a mess. Thus, it's better to start drawing while your projects are still small. My recommendation is to draw diagrams as often as you can, mostly to train yourself to visualize the software you create. It's a very vital skill that so many programmers are lacking.

Use cases are also known as *functional requirements* (FRs). Any system may also have *non-functional requirements* (NFRs) that are not related to the way we use the system, but to the quality of the system. This is why they are sometimes called *quality requirements*. For example, nobody will want to play our game if it's very slow. Like if a User hits the [　　] button and the Bullet is fired in 200 milliseconds or more. Such a delay in reaction to the User's actions would be unacceptable. However, our functional requirements don't say anything about it. We may implement them fully, but the system won't be useful and our customer won't pay for it. Thus, the scope is not complete if it misses quality requirements. Let's add these few, for responsibility, interoperability, and maintainability (together known as *-ilities*):

```
Q1: The response time for all User's actions must be
    less than 5ms.
Q2: The System must work on Safari, Chrome,
    IE, and Firefox.
Q3: The source code must be clean and easy to read.
```

By adding these new, non-functional requirements, we introduced *ambiguity* to our requirements specification document. Seriously, should Q1 be true on any possible computer? With any speed of Internet connection? With any amount of software programs running in the background? Will Q2 be true if we use Internet Explorer 3 or one of the first versions of Firefox, which didn't

142

support many of the modern features of JavaScript? What exactly does "easy to read" in Q3 mean? Easy for who? To get rid of this ambiguity, the requirements have to be *refined*. How about these requirements instead:

```
Q1: The response time for all User's actions must be
    less than 5ms, on a 1.7GHz+ computer with 8Gb+ RAM,
    with no CPU-intensive programs in the background.
Q2: The System must work on Safari 10+, Chrome 60+,
    IE 10+, and Firefox 65+.
Q3: The source code must ESLint compliant.
```

Ambiguity is the most hurtful disease of all requirement documents, and one of the most dangerous enemies of all software projects. When we don't know what exactly to do, how can we do it right? And knowing exactly what needs to be done is usually impossible or very difficult. Even the second attempt made above with the quality requirements is not perfect. We didn't say what exactly are CPU-intensive programs; how many CPUs must be available; how fast the disk system must be; how fast the network connection is; and so on. We didn't say anything about the plugins any of these web browsers may have installed; they may also seriously affect the performance of our game and even the functionality of it. We didn't give the version of ESLint and didn't specify the exact set of rules to be configured in it.

We may keep refining our requirements for many iterations, making them better and better, but usually we don't want to do that. We have to stop at some point and say "enough." However, I don't think that having some requirements is better than not having anything—this doesn't sound right to me. A bad requirements document may certainly kill the project, especially if the team doesn't have the courage or motivation to doubt the document and suggest something different. But aiming for a perfectly unambiguous set of requirements is definitely a false objective.

★★
What is the difference between use cases and *user stories*?

★★
Diagram drawing could be called a *soft skill*. Name five other soft skills a good software engineer must posses.

★★
Read *Writing Effective Use Cases (2000)* by Cockburn [3].

★★
Specify the requirement no.2 in a full use case format.

★★
Name at least five qualities of a properly specified requirement, according to IEEE 29148:2018 standard.

★★
Read *Software Requirements (2013)* by Wiegers and Beatty [20].

★★★
Name ten non-functional requirements and suggest their specification texts for our web app.

★★★
Specify requirements in the format suggested above for a mobile dating app similar to Tinder.

4.2 Architecture

Now, when we know what to do, it's time to define the architecture of our system. Good software engineers use three UML diagrams to document the architecture of any object-oriented system: *object diagram, component diagram*, and *deployment diagram*. There are many other diagrams in UML, but they will be helpful later at the lower levels of the system, when we start creating objects and connecting them together.

Let's start with the object diagram. Usually, this one is the one that takes most of the time and effort to create. Deciding which objects will participate in the system and what the best names for them are is a very complex problem to solve. For our game, I decided to create five objects:

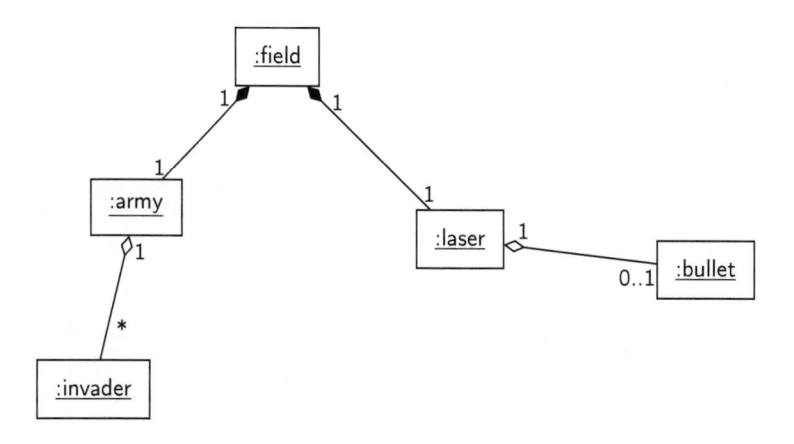

Figure 4.2: UML Object Diagram of Space Invaders

Three of them will exist in only one instance, like `field`, `army`, and `laser`. The `bullet` may or may not exist, while the `invader`(s) may be present in many instances. Having this information, you may guess what those lines, numbers, and symbols mean on the diagram above. The `field` is the abstraction of the entire game; the `army` is the entire group of Invaders; the `laser` is the device the User moves left and right to point the gun; and `bullet`(s) and `invader`(s) are the flying objects on the screen. Sometimes objects on the diagram may also have methods and attributes, but I wouldn't recommend doing that. The purpose of a diagram is not to give explicit instructions to programmers on how to write code and which methods to have in every particular object. Instead, the purpose of an object diagram is to highlight the most important elements of the design and convey the core idea of *object decomposition* in the system. The diagram may include only a limited subset of all of the objects. There's no need to make it very detailed and exactly match the source code. The diagram is a message to other programmers, not a technical specification of the software product.

The next diagram defines which *components* our system will be divided into. A classic definition of a component is a *runtime* structure, while objects are *static* structures. Objects are static because they are elements of the source code, which is not running, but is edited by programmers. Components, on the other hand, are working in runtime and being executed by CPUs. Components usually communicate with each other via the network, but it can also be POSIX interprocess communication (IPC) interfaces or anything else. I would suggest identifying the following three components in our game:

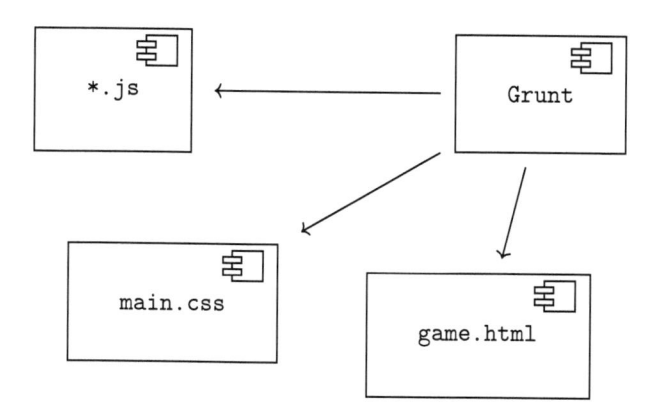

Figure 4.3: UML Component Diagram of Space Invaders

Here, `*.js` is a collection of all JavaScript objects; `main.css` is the CSS stylesheet; `game.html` is the main and the only HTML file in the project; and `Grunt` is the build automated via Grunt, using `Gruntfile`.

Finally, this is the deployment diagram, which demonstrates where our components will work in which runtime environments, after we *deploy* them. The boxes on the diagram are the environments.

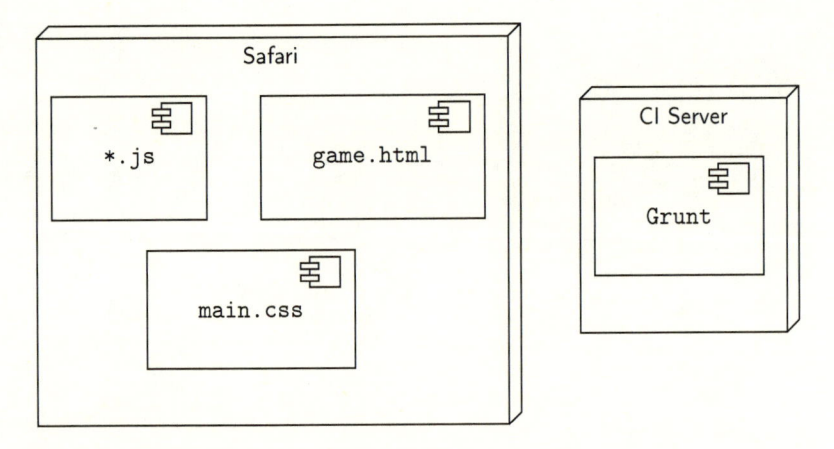

Figure 4.4: UML Deployment Diagram of Space Invaders

Here, `CI Server` is the continuous integration server that is supposed to build the project, put pieces together, and prepare it for our User, who will play the game in their Safari web browser.

No matter how small the software product is, it is recommended to always start the development of it with these three diagrams. We must identify the most important objects, components, and runtime environments. We must find out how they are connected and what the dependencies between them are. Obviously, it's recommended to keep the diagrams up to date during the course of the projects. There is nothing more annoying in software development than inconsistencies between documentation and the source code.

★
Why are object names on the diagram underscored and prepended with a colon?

★★
What is the difference between a class diagram and an object diagram?

★★
Explain the purpose of CSS stylesheets and give five examples of CSS styles our game may benefit from.

★★
How would the meaning of the object diagram change if we removed cardinality markers (`1`, `0..1` and `*`)?

★★
Suggest three tools for UML drawings.

★★
Explain what *reverse engineering* is.

★★
Suggest three tools that take the source code and generate UML diagrams.

★★
Read *The Mythical Man-Month (1995)* by Brooks Jr [2].

★★★
What is the difference between association and inheritance arrows in a UML class diagram?

★★★
Draw an activity diagram of our game.

★★★
Pass the OMG Certified UML Professional (OCUP) exam and get a certificate.

4.3 Design

There are two approaches to design in any software application: bottom-up and top-down. The first one means making smaller lower-level pieces first, and then assembling them into larger parts until the entire application is ready. If we made a car in bottom-up style, we would first make nuts and bolts, then pieces of the engine, make the wheels, assemble the engine, make the body, and finally put all of the parts together to make the car. This is actually how cars are made. However, this is not how professional software engineers work. Instead, we start from the body ... actually, we don't even start with the body. We start with the car.

We build something that works, and we do it as fast as we can. Then, we see where the problems are and we fix them. Then we go deeper and fix lower-level problems. Ultimately, we replace the horse with an engine and the customer is happy. Indeed, if we used the automobile metaphor, the first version of a software product may look like a car with one wheel and a donkey instead of an engine. It would also look ugly, have no seats, and move backwards. However, it would be able to take a customer from point A to point B, just in a very inconvenient way.

Then, the next release would make our Frankenstein's Monster look nicer, have two wheels instead of one, and move forward. The third release would make it even better, and so on. It would never be perfect; we would always have issues and things to fix. This is how software development works—it is never finished. Every next release makes our product better and maybe even adds new features.

The top-down design may also be called "customer first" design because we think about customers before we think about our own technical interests. We want to deliver a working product or a feature, first of all. How technically sound it will be upon implementation is our second concern. Everything we do must be focused on delivering the functionality to our users. Most programmers misunderstand this concept because they are afraid of disappointing the customer with something that doesn't work. They believe that the customer will not like the car with one wheel and a donkey instead of an engine. I understand the caution ... that ruined so many projects. Software engineering is not the same as making cars or building houses. In software development, we have the luxury of being able to deliver fast, even when the product is not fully ready. We can't do the same with houses or cars, unfortunately. On the other hand, software development is a much more risky process since customer requirements are usually much more vague and volatile. Having these two factors in mind, we have to do our best to deliver as soon as the product in our hands is deliverable. How correct it is must not be of our concern ... at the particular release we are shipping.

Of course, we must help our customers understand the strategy. They must be prepared that we may send them a single-wheeled car. They must understand that the software development process is incremental, and every next version of the same software product will have improvements. They just need to have patience and motivation to politely criticize our mistakes. We, on the other hand, must record their feedback and make fixes in next releases. This is how true incremental development and delivery of a software product must work.

Thus, let's start with a moving Laser to let the client play the game. First, we need HTML with the field and the Laser:

```html
<!DOCTYPE html>
<html>
  <head>
    <script src='src/main.js'></script>
  </head>
  <body onload="field.init(document);">
    <section id="field">
      <div id="laser"
        style="position:absolute;bottom:0;">xxx</div>
    </section>
  </body>
</html>
```

There are two elements with `id` attributes: `<section>` and `<div>`. The attribute `onload` in the body contains a short JavaScript statement to be executed right after the HTML page is loaded in a browser. It executes the method `init()` of the object `field`. The `document` variable, which we pass there as a single argument, is defined in each web browser and is part of Document Object Model (DOM) specification. In other words, every browser will have such variable defined somewhere deep inside it. We don't know how and where it's defined, we just know what methods it has (they are named in the DOM specification). Here is how I would define the object `field` and its single method in the file `main.js`:

```
const field = {
  init: function(doc) {
    doc.addEventListener(
      'keydown',
      function(evt) {
        if (evt.keyCode === 37) {
          field.move_laser(doc, -15);
        }
        if (evt.keyCode === 39) {
          field.move_laser(doc, +15);
        }
      }
    );
  },
  move_laser: function(doc, dx) {
    const div = doc.getElementById('laser');
    const rect = div.getBoundingClientRect();
    div.style.left = rect.left + dx + 'px';
  }
};
```

Try to put this code into your browser and take a note of what you see. The game will be there. You will be able to move the Laser left and right. You won't be able to shoot any Bullets; you will not see the Invaders; and you won't be able to win or lose. You will see a car with a single wheel. However, it will look like a game that's deliverable to a customer.

Let's see what this code does. The HTML part is simple, except, maybe the `style` attribute, which positions the Laser at the bottom of the viewpoint. Such a positioning is required to make it possible to move it freely to any place. A more interesting part is the `field` object, which has two methods: `init()` and `move_laser`.

The method `init()` instructs the object `doc`, which it receives as a single argument, what to do when the User hits any key on their keyboard. When it happens, the anonymous function, which is provided as a second argument of `addEventListener()`, will be executed and will receive the object `evt` as its single argument. It will be an object with pre-set attributes that we can read. The attribute we are interested in is `keyCode`. Its value represents the Unicode symbol on the keyboard: `37` for `←` and `39` for `→`. If the left-key is pressed, we ask the `field` to `move_laser` by -15 pixels, and if the right-key is pressed, by +15 pixels.

The method `move_laser` finds the `<div>` element in the DOM document `doc` and resets its coordinates by the required difference, directly modifying the attribute `left` of the attribute `style` of the object `div`. This, according to each and every expert of object-oriented programming, is terrible practice. However, this is how DOM specification was designed in 1998 (it's very likely its authors were not big fans of OOP). An object must encapsulate attributes and never let anyone from the outside touch them. More powerful programming languages, like Java or C++, make it possible to *protect* attributes against such intrusive behavior. However, JavaScript doesn't have this ability, and any object can touch any attributes of any other object.

There is one more type of UML diagrams you may want to use while designing your software: *sequence diagrams* (time goes from top to bottom in all parallel threads). They help us understand the interaction between different objects and components. Here is what the process of `field` initialization may look like in such a diagram:

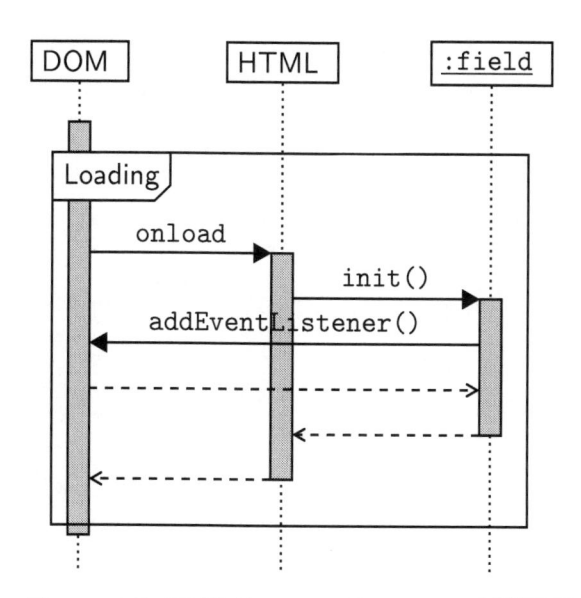

Figure 4.5: UML Sequence Diagram of `field`

This is what the interaction between DOM of the browser and two functional parts of the object `field` may look like:

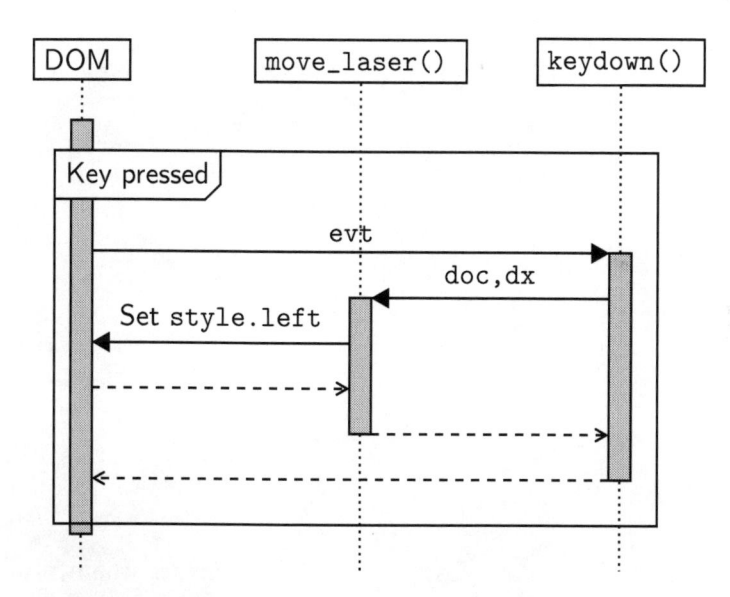

Figure 4.6: UML Sequence Diagram of `laser`

Sequence diagrams are not mandatory, but they may greatly help in visualizing the software you design. In the modern software world, writing code is just a small part of the job programmers do. A much larger part is explaining to other programmers how the code works and helping them maintain it. In most cases, diagrams convey design decisions much faster and better than thousands of lines of code. Some software experts may argue that the code must be written in such a way that no diagrams are required to understand it, and they would be right. However, such perfect code never exists in real life. Moreover, when the development progresses, the quality of the code usually goes down, complexity increases, and readability drops. Without diagrams, which we usually create when the project is still young, the team will be having a hard time understanding the architecture in a few months or years.

★
What is `<!DOCTYPE html>` at the top of our HTML file for?

★
What is the code of the `return` key?

★★
Similar to `evt`, suggest five other *abbreviations* for `event`.

★★
What is `position:absolute` in the HTML code above used for?

★★
Name five other types of DOM events that we can pass to `addEventListener()`.

★★
What will happen if you pass `'abcdef'` as the first argument of `addEventListener()` in the code above?

★★
What will be returned by `getElementById('laser')` if the HTML page has more than one element with the `id` equal to `'laser'`?

★★
Explain how it's possible to add a number to a number and then to a string in the `rect.left+dx+'px'` line above.

★★
Explain why `37` stands for `←` and `39` stands for `→`.

★★
Make the Laser stop when it hits the left or the right border of the screen.

★★
Compare inheritance, composition, and aggregation and explain the pros and cons of each one.

★★
Make the Laser also move up and down.

★★
Explain the difference between Architecture and Design.

★★
Read *Clean Code (2009)* by Martin [14].

★★
Read my blog post: *Encapsulation Covers Up Naked Data (2016)*.

4.4 Refactoring

Even though the JavaScript code we wrote works, it's far from perfect. It can be improved in order to become cleaner and more readable. For example, we can *extract* the method `move_laser` from the `field` and make a new object `laser` out of it:

```
const laser = {
  move: function(doc, dx) {
    const div = doc.getElementById('laser');
    const rect = div.getBoundingClientRect();
    div.style.left = rect.left + dx + 'px';
  }
};
const field = {
  init: function(doc) {
    doc.addEventListener(
      'keydown',
      function(evt) {
        if (evt.keyCode === 37) {
          laser.move(doc, -15);
        }
        if (evt.keyCode === 39) {
          laser.move(doc, +15);
        }
      }
    );
  },
};
```

Now the code looks better because we have two smaller objects, `laser` and `field`, instead of a single larger one. However, we can still make it better. Now, both variables `laser` and `field` are *global* ones, which means that they are visible to all objects. Global variables are considered to be bad practice in OOP and in a perfect software, there should only be one global variable that represents the entire application. The variable `field` is a good candidate for such a global variable. It represents the entire playground of the application. The `laser` has to be be encapsulate in the `field`, just like our object diagram demonstrated earlier. We can do it easily:

158

```
const field = {
  laser: {
    move: function(doc, dx) {
      const div = doc.getElementById('laser');
      const rect = div.getBoundingClientRect();
      div.style.left = rect.left + dx + 'px';
    }
  },
  init: function(doc) {
    doc.addEventListener(
      'keydown',
      function(evt) {
        if (evt.keyCode === 37) {
          this.laser.move(doc, -15);
        }
        if (evt.keyCode === 39) {
          this.laser.move(doc, +15);
        }
      }
    );
  },
};
```

Pay attention to the usage of `this.laser` in the anonymous function. In this snippet, the `laser` is an attribute of `field`, not a global variable anymore. That's why it has to be referred to as `this.laser` and can only be accessible from within the `field`. In JavaScript, it's possible to access it from the outside, like this, too:

```
field.laser.move(d, 10);
```

But this is bad practice and I strongly discourage you from doing so. Attributes are only supposed to be used inside their owners.

The next step of possible *refactoring* (modifying the code in order to make it better without changing its functionality) is the *introduction* of constructors. At the moment, neither the `field` nor the `laser` have constructors. This makes it necessary to pass all required objects as arguments of their methods. For example, the method `move()` expects two arguments while the first one is the DOM document, which will always be the same. It would be more convenient if the `laser` knew about the document during its (the `laser`) entire lifetime. Let's add constructors to both of them:

```
function laser(d) {
  return {
    doc: d,
    move: function(dx) {
      const div = this.doc.getElementById('laser');
      const rect = div.getBoundingClientRect();
      div.style.left = rect.left + dx + 'px';
    }
  };
}
function field(d) {
  return {
    doc: d,
    laser: laser(d),
    init: function() {
      this.doc.addEventListener(
        'keydown',
        function(evt) {
          if (evt.keyCode === 37) {
            this.laser.move(-15);
          }
          if (evt.keyCode === 39) {
            this.laser.move(+15);
          }
        }.bind(this)
      );
    }
  };
}
```

Now, the HTML part should look like this:

```
<body onload="field(document).init();">
```

You may wonder why we use the same names for constructors as we used for the variables. The name of the variable was `laser` and now the constructor is called `laser()`. On top of that, the attribute of the `field` is also called `laser`. Here is the logic: when we didn't have constructors, we had a standalone variable `laser` and it was the only Laser in the application. Hence the name. Now, we have a constructor and it's the only constructor that can create a Laser; that's why its name is `laser()`. The name of the attribute follows the same logic: it's the only Laser in the entire `field`, hence the name "laser."

If we would explain the code we have now in a UML object diagram, it would look like this:

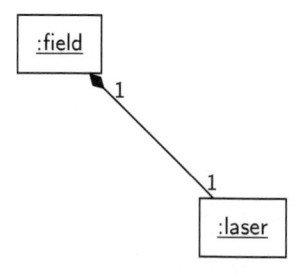

Figure 4.7: UML Object Diagram, Updated

This isn't the entire system, but it's something we can call a working piece of software and deliver it to the customer. The beauty of refactoring is that it can be done endlessly. No matter how clean and elegant the code is, there are still many places for improvement. In the code above, I would delegate the configuration of the DOM event handler to the `laser`. Now the `field` is doing it, while the dispatching of User's actions is entirely the responsibility of the Laser. Thus, this is the refactoring we can make:

```
function laser(d) {
  return {
    doc: d,
    move: function(dx) { /* No changes */ },
    init: function() {
      this.doc.addEventListener(
        'keydown',
        function(evt) {
          if (evt.keyCode === 37) {
            this.move(-15);
          }
          if (evt.keyCode === 39) {
            this.move(+15);
          }
        }.bind(this)
      );
    }
  };
}
function field(d) {
  return {
    doc: d,
    laser: laser(d),
    init: function() {
      this.laser.init();
    }
  };
}
```

Once `field.init()` is called, it redirects the call to `this.laser.init()`, which does the event dispatcher configuration through the DOM method `addEventListener()`.

★
Why do constructor argument names differ from the names of object attributes, even though they point to the same object? For example `laser(d)` and `laser.doc`.

★★
Explain why global variables are bad practice.

★★
Explain how global variables caused problems for Toyota™ in 2013.

★★
Read *Refactoring: Improving the Design of Existing Code (2018)* by Fowler [6].

★★
Name three other refactorings, aside from "introducing a constructor," and explain how they work.

4.5 Integration Test

Now, since our product is ready to be shipped to the "customer," we must, as we discussed in Section 3.3, cover it with unit tests to make sure our primitive functionality actually works. It should work not only in our own Safari when we open the `game.html` file, but also in the automated build. We should run `grunt` and be able to test the functionality of both `laser` and `field`. Does method `move()` actually move the Laser left and right? Does `field` actually configure the DOM to react on `←` and `→`? Does `move()` move to the required amount of pixels?

Here is what our test may look like to validate that `move()`

actually moves:

```
const mocha = require('mocha');
const assert = require('assert');
mocha.describe('laser', function() {
  mocha.it('moves itself left', function() {
    laser(document).move(+10);
    const div = document.getElementById('laser');
    const rect = div.getBoundingClientRect();
    assert.equal(10, rect.left);
  });
});
```

In the first two lines, as we did before, we load two libraries to help us write the unit test. In the body of the test we:
1) Instantiate a Laser object using `laser()` constructor; 2) Call the method `move()`, asking the Laser to move itself right ten pixels; 3) Take the HTML element from the `document`; and
4) Compare the coordinate of its left side with the expected number `10` (this code is very similar or even identical to what we already have in the method `move()`).

It looks like a great test, but it won't work simply because there is no such thing as variable `document` as long as there is no real browser. The global variable `document` is provided by the DOM implementation, which is inside Safari (or another browser). When we run our tests from the command line using Grunt, Safari is not involved. But the variable `document` is required since it has to be passed into the `laser()` constructor, as it's the only argument. Where can we get it?

The first option, as we discussed in Section 3.4, is to mock this variable. Mocking is a great technique when variables are simple. However, in this case, we will have to mock the entire DOM, which includes hundreds of types and thousands of methods. Even mocking the functionality of `document`, which we use in `move()`, would take hours of work and will make the code of the unit test very complex and unreadable. This is not an option in this case, and when mocking is not an option, we use *integration tests*.

The only, key difference between unit tests and integration tests is that unit tests always use mocks in order to break dependencies.

An integration test, which we will create right now, will use what is called a "headless" version of a web browser (we will use Firefox). We will use Karma, a JavaScript framework, which is configured in the `Gruntfile.js`. Karma starts Firefox, injects our JavaScript files into it, and runs all of the tests. Then, when all of the tests are finished, it shuts down Firefox, collects the results, and breaks the build if any issues were found. The browser is called "headless" because it doesn't really start its main window. It works, but the developer doesn't see it. Here is how it has to be configured in `Gruntfile.js` (it's only a piece of the configuration, but the most important one):

```
module.exports = function(grunt) {
  grunt.initConfig({
    karma: {
      unit: {
        options: {
          files: ['test/**/*.js', 'src/**/*.js'],
        },
        frameworks: ['assert', 'mocha'],
        port: 9876,
        browsers: ['FirefoxHeadless']
      },
    },
  });
  grunt.loadNpmTasks('grunt-karma');
};
```

In the `files`, we instruct Karma where to get the
files to be injected into Firefox. In `frameworks`,
we inform it which frameworks to also inject there.
The `port` is the TCP port number `9876`, which
will be used by Firefox to communicate with Karma, and
`browsers` is the list of browsers to use. The source code of the
test has to be changed in order to work inside Firefox:

```
describe('laser', function() {
  it('moves itself left', function() {
    document.body.innerHTML = '<div style="' +
      'left:100px;position:absolute;" ' +
      'id="laser">xxx</div>';
    laser(document).move(+10);
    const div = document.getElementById('laser');
    const rect = div.getBoundingClientRect();
    assert.equal(110, rect.left);
  });
});
```

There are two important modifications compared to the previous version. First, we set the body of `innerHTML` of the DOM `document` before letting Laser move itself. This is not the real playground we have in our `game.html` HTML file, but it's good enough to run the test. The Laser will find itself in the HTML by the `id` and will move it. Second, we don't do `require()` anymore, but use `describe()` and `it()` directly, as if they are globally visible. They are indeed globally visible thanks to Karma; it injected them into Firefox on start because we asked it to do so in the `frameworks` configuration option inside `Gruntfile.js`.

It is now required to have Firefox installed to let Karma use it. Karma knows how to find it in the system, but it has to be installed and its version should be fresh enough, otherwise Karma may complain and fail the build.

Integration tests are usually much slower than unit tests since they need additional heavyweight *scaffolding*. Every time we run Grunt, Firefox has to start, which may take a few seconds or maybe even a dozen seconds. Then, Karma communicates with Firefox through HTTP over TCP to tell Firefox what to do. This interaction is pretty fast since both Grunt+Karma and Firefox are at the same computer, but still much slower than a simple method call from one JavaScript object to another.

Usually, in larger software projects, we have both unit and integration tests. The amount of unit tests is usually much larger, while the total time of their execution is much shorter. If all of your unit tests combined take more than a minute to complete, something is wrong with their design or the project is too large and you just have too many unit tests. If this is the case, you'd better break your project into smaller ones. Large code bases is a problem, not something to be proud of.

★★
Try to find JavaScript libraries that make an attempt to mock DOM.

★★
Explain how *test fixtures* help make tests more readable.

★★
Some experts believe that large "monolithic" code repositories is the right way to design software products. Why do they think so? What are their arguments?

★★
Read *Growing Object-Oriented Software, Guided by Tests (2009)* by Freeman and Pryce [7].

★ ★ ★
Explain the relationship between HTTP, TCP, and IP.

★ ★ ★
Exactly how many types and methods are in DOM specification?

4.6 DRY

If we look at the body of the `laser` and the integration test we just created, it will be obvious that they do the same thing: getting the horizontal coordinate of the Laser. I'm talking about these thee lines of code in the `move()` method:

```
const div = document.getElementById('laser');
const rect = div.getBoundingClientRect();
div.style.left = rect.left + dx + 'px';
```

The integration test has very similar another three lines:

```
const div = document.getElementById('laser');
const rect = div.getBoundingClientRect();
assert.equal(110, rect.left);
```

The only difference between these two snippets is in how they use the coordinates they retrieve from the `rect.left`. This is called *code duplication*, and it's one of the biggest sins in software engineering. The main reason why it's a bad practice is that we don't want programmers to remember all of the places to make changes when they're required. If we leave our two snippets the way they are, sooner or later we may decide to make some changes and we may forget that we have to make them in two places. We will only change one place and the second one will remain untouched. This will cause an inconsistency in the source code, and eventually it will cause a maintainability problem. Long story short, we must not write even a single line of code twice.

How do we get rid of this duplication? I think we can introduce a new method `x()` in the object `laser`, which will return the coordinates of the Laser:

```
function laser(d) {
  return {
    doc: d,
    x: function() {
      const div = this.doc.getElementById('laser');
      const rect = div.getBoundingClientRect();
      return rect.left;
    },
    move: function(dx) {
      const div = this.doc.getElementById('laser');
      div.style.left = this.x() + dx + 'px';
    }
  };
}
```

The test will become shorter:

```
describe('laser', function() {
  it('moves itself left', function() {
    document.body.innerHTML = '<div style="' +
      'left:100px;position:absolute;" ' +
      'id="laser">xxx</div>';
    const lz = laser(document);
    lz.move(+10);
    assert.equal(110, lz.x());
  });
});
```

You may notice that we still have code duplication in both methods `x()` and `move()` with this identical line:

```
const div = this.doc.getElementById('laser');
```

In order to resolve this issue, we may want to introduce a new method `div()`:

```
function laser(d) {
  return {
    doc: d,
    div: function() {
      return this.doc.getElementById('laser');
    },
    x: function() {
      return this.div().getBoundingClientRect().left;
    },
    move: function(dx) {
      this.div().style.left = this.x() + dx + 'px';
    }
  };
}
```

Now our object looks great. There is no code duplication, and the methods are very short. In general, it's a virtue. The shorter the method, the better. Also, pay attention to the method names. Methods `x()` and `div()` are returning something and their names are nouns. The method `move()` doesn't return anything, but it does make some modifications to other objects. Its name is a verb. It's good practice to separate object methods into two categories: *builders* like `div()`, and *manipulators* like `move()`.

★ ★
Why this Section is called DRY?

★ ★
Add an element to the top right corner of the game page with the current value of the Laser x coordinate and make sure it changes when the Laser moves.

★★
Make sure the User can't move the Laser outside of the game field; neither too far right nor too far left.

★★
Add a CSS stylesheet to the document and make sure the Laser looks like a black bar that's 60x20 pixels.

★★
Read *Working Effectively with Legacy Code (2004)* by Feathers [4].

★★
Read my blog post: *Builders and Manipulators (2018)*.

4.7 Concurrency

Let's add the Army of Invaders, who will show up automatically and will move from left to right and then backwards, slowly getting down, until one of them touches the Laser and the game is over. There will be two new objects: `army` and `invader`. The `army` will belong to the `field`:

```
function field(w) {
  return {
    window: w,
    laser: laser(w),
    army: army(w), // Here!
    init: function() {
      this.laser.init();
      this.army.init(); // And here!
    },
  };
}
```

The method `init()`, which is called by DOM's `onload` event, makes two consecutive calls to two methods `init()` in two encapsulated objects, and then quits. Then later, another DOM event `onkeydown` arrives, and the anonymous function registered in the method `laser.init()` is triggered. Visually, on a sequence diagram it looks like this (DOM_1 and DOM_2 are two different execution *threads* inside DOM):

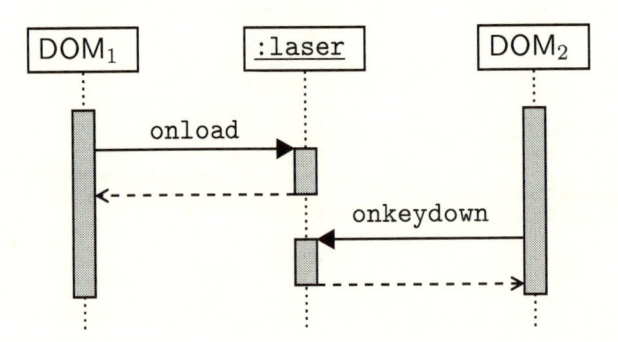

Figure 4.8: UML Sequence Diagram of Laser

The `laser` object is called from two different places. The first time, it's called by DOM when the document is loaded, thanks to the HTML attribute `onload`:

```
<body onload="field.init(window);">
  <!-- everything else -->
</body>
```

The second time, it's called when the User hits any key on the keyboard, and the control is given to the anonymous function registered inside `init()`:

```
init: function() {
  this.doc.addEventListener('keydown', function(evt) {
    if (evt.keyCode === 37) {
      this.move(-15);
    }
    if (evt.keyCode === 39) {
      this.move(+15);
    }
  }.bind(this));
}
```

Thus, there are two clients of the `laser` and they work parallel to each other: DOM_1 and DOM_2. We don't know when exactly they will interact with the `laser` because the `laser` has no control over them. They belong to the browser. Moreover, they may interact with the `laser` concurrently. Imagine a situation where the User hits the button and the anonymous listener is triggered. The `laser` starts processing the request, and while the processing is still not finished, the User hits another button. The listener will be triggered again while the previous one is still working. They will work *concurrently*, like this:

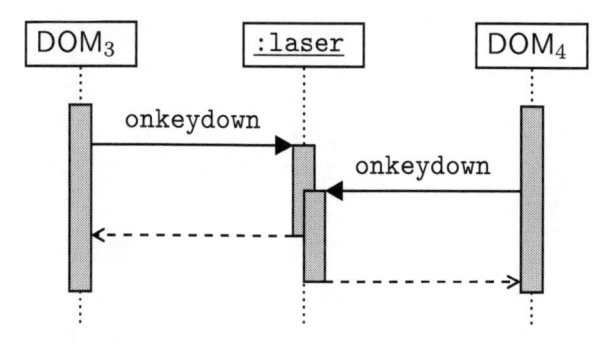

Figure 4.9: UML Sequence Diagram of Laser demonstrating how concurrency works

In order to make the *concurrency* possible, the client must be *multi-threaded*; instead of one *thread*, it has to have a number a threads. A "thread of execution" is like a smaller CPU inside a larger one that works on something specific. For example, one thread may watch the keyboard and when the User hits a button, call the `laser`, while another thread may watch the clock and at the right moment of time ask the `army` to put a new Invader on the screen:

```
function army(w) {
  return {
    window: w,
    invaders: 0,
    init: function() {
      this.launch(10000);
    },
    launch: function(delay) {
      const i = invader(this.window, this.invaders++);
      i.launch();
      this.window.setTimeout(function() {
        this.launch(delay - 50);
      }.bind(this), delay);
    },
  };
}
```

The method `init()` is called by the `field` when the `army` has to be initialized for the first time. The `army` calls the method `launch` with a single argument: the amount of milliseconds to wait between placing new Invaders to the screen (10 seconds in the example above). The method `launch()` creates a new `invader`, launches it, and asks DOM through `this.window` to start watching the clock. Calling `setTimeout(f, m)` with two parameters literally means "trigger this anonymous function `f` in `m` milliseconds". A new thread starts on the DOM side and keeps watching the clock. At the right moment, it calls the provided anonymous function.

The anonymous function will call `launch()` again, but with a decremented argument `delay`. Thus, every time we launch a new Invader, we *recursively* ask ourselves to do it again, but a bit faster every next time.

Most programming languages have very limited tools for organizing concurrency. Most of them, like JavaScript, don't know anything about it, but only third-party libraries and frameworks help their users organize threads, just like the functionality of `setTimeout()` provided by DOM did it for us. Very often they are not really third-party and are designed by the same company or the same group of people, but they are not built into the language itself.

The most typical and critical problem related to concurrency is the so called *thread-safety* and *race condition*, which happens when it's absent. Take a look at the `laser` code once again, especially at the part where we move it:

```
move: function(dx) {
  this.div().style.left = this.x() + dx + 'px';
}
```

If this method is called from one thread, everything is fine. However, if many different threads try to move the Laser left and right, the final position of it will not be determined. This code, if being executed from a single thread, will move the Laser to the right by +25 pixels:

```
laser.move(+10);
laser.move(+20);
laser.move(-15);
laser.move(+10);
```

However, if exactly the same thing is done from four different threads at the same time, the position will be ... unpredictable because of the race condition. The reading of the position of the

Laser and updating it are *decoupled* in time, and another updating or reading operation may happen between them. Technically, the four moves mentioned above work like this:

```
1.1: read x
1.2: save x + 10
2.1: read x
2.2: save x + 20
3.1: read x
3.2: save x - 15
4.1: read x
4.2: save x + 10
```

When these instructions are executed consequently, the result is predictable; but if we do them simultaneously, we may end up with this (or something similar):

```
1.1: read x
2.1: read x
1.2: save x + 10
3.1: read x
4.1: read x
2.2: save x + 20
3.2: save x - 15
4.2: save x + 10
```

The result will be $+20$ instead of the expected $+25$. And it's impossible to predict its exact value since the instructions may be tossed differently when we run our four threads next time. Race condition is one of the hardest problems to solve in programming. It's almost impossible to solve it via debugging or unit testing. The only way to solve it is by reviewing the code and making some blocks of it thread-safe, which means adding *exclusive locking* for sensitive blocks of code:

```
move: function(dx) {
  // Lock
  this.div().style.left = this.x() + dx + 'px';
  // Unlock
}
```

Here, at the "lock" line we get an exclusive status for the current thread and ask all other threads to wait until we "unlock." How exactly this lock/unlock functionality will be implemented depends on the programming language. For example, Java has a built-in `synchronized` keyword for it and we can do something like this (this is Java code):

```java
void move() {
  synchronized (this) {
    left = this.x() + dx;
  }
}
```

With this locking introduced, the method `move()` is thread-safe. No matter how many threads call it simultaneously, its behavior won't change, and the final result is always predictable.

Let's implement the `invader` and use `setTimeout()` one more time to make each Invader active and move on its own, from left to right and from top to bottom:

```
function invader(w, i) {
  return {
    window: w,
    id: 'invader' + i,
    launch: function() {
      const div = this.window.document
        .createElement('div');
      div.id = this.id;
      div.className = 'invader';
      this.window.document.getElementById('field')
        .appendChild(div);
      this.attack(40, 2);
    },
    attack: function(v, dx) {
      const div = this.window.document
        .getElementById(this.id);
      const rect = div.getBoundingClientRect();
      const x = rect.left + dx;
      div.style.left = x + 'px';
      this.window.setTimeout(function() {
        const width = div.parentElement
          .getBoundingClientRect().width;
        if (x > width - rect.width || x < 0) {
          div.style.top =
             rect.top + rect.height * 2 + 'px';
          this.attack(v - 1, -dx);
        } else {
          this.attack(v, dx);
        }
      }.bind(this), v);
    },
  };
}
```

To make Invaders work I had to create a CSS stylesheet `main.css` and attach it to the HTML:

```
.invader {
  position: absolute;
  top: 10px;
  left: 10px;
  width: 40px;
  height: 10px;
  background-color: firebrick;
}
```

This is the modification I had to make to the HTML:

```
<head>
  <link type='text/css'
    href='css/main.css' rel='stylesheet'/>
</head>
```

The logic of `invader` is simple. First, it is launched via the method `launch()`, which creates a new DOM element of type `div`; sets two attributes, `id` and `className`; and appends it to the existing DOM element `field`. Then, it calls the method `attack()`, which finds the current location of the Invader's `div` in the DOM and moves it left or right by the `dx` pixels. Finally, it uses `setTimeout()` to call itself recursively in a few milliseconds and shift the `div` again.

★
What do you think will happen if we replace `this.invaders++` with `++this.invaders`?

★★
Why do we use `window` instead of `document` from now on?

★★
Why it was necessary to use CSS in order to make Invaders work?

★★
Make the Invaders have random speed when they start and then add random acceleration.

★ ★

Explain why two listeners will never be triggered by the DOM of a web browser at the same time, and will always be triggered one by one, consequently.

★ ★

Read *Java Concurrency in Practice (2006)* by Goetz et al. [8].

★ ★ ★

Get rid of `setTimeout()` and use JavaScript *promises*.

★ ★ ★

Implement methods `lock()` and `unlock()` for our JavaScript project.

4.8 Design Patterns

Let's check the status of the scope of our project using a *requirements traceability matrix*. It's a simple table with a full list of requirements that we introduced in the Section 4.1, and a list of implementation elements, like objects and components:

	R1: Move the Laser	R2: Fire Bullets	R3: Place Invaders	R4: Destroy an Invader	R5: Stop the Game
`field`	✓	?	✓	?	?
`laser`	✓	?			
`army`			✓		
`invader`			✓		
`bullet`		?		?	
`main.css`			✓		
`game.html`	✓	?	✓	?	?
`Gruntfile`					

Usually, this matrix is used to map requirements to test cases and demonstrate that we successfully covered everything the customer wants with the tests performed by testers. I believe the matrix can be used for other things too, like checking the scope and validating the necessity of every implementation element. In the matrix, we can easily understand what our objects and components are for and make sure we didn't make them for no reason.

The check mark ✓ in the table means that the component on the left was definitely made to satisfy the requirement on the top. The question mark means that we still don't know because the component is not yet implemented, but we predict it to be made for the requirement on the top. An empty cell means that the component was definitely not made specifically for the requirement on the top.

What does this table demonstrate to us? First, there is an empty row with `Gruntfile`. This means that we have the component, but nobody required us to make it. In business language, nobody paid us to create it. Why did we do it? For ourselves, in order to automate the development and deployment. It's a great goal, but it's better to avoid *gold platting*, which is implementing anything that is not *in scope*. We must add a new requirement to the scope and a new actor: a programmer. Of course, in a real project we would have to approve the changes via an officially submitted *change request*, and the project would have to be re-estimated. Here is a new use case diagram:

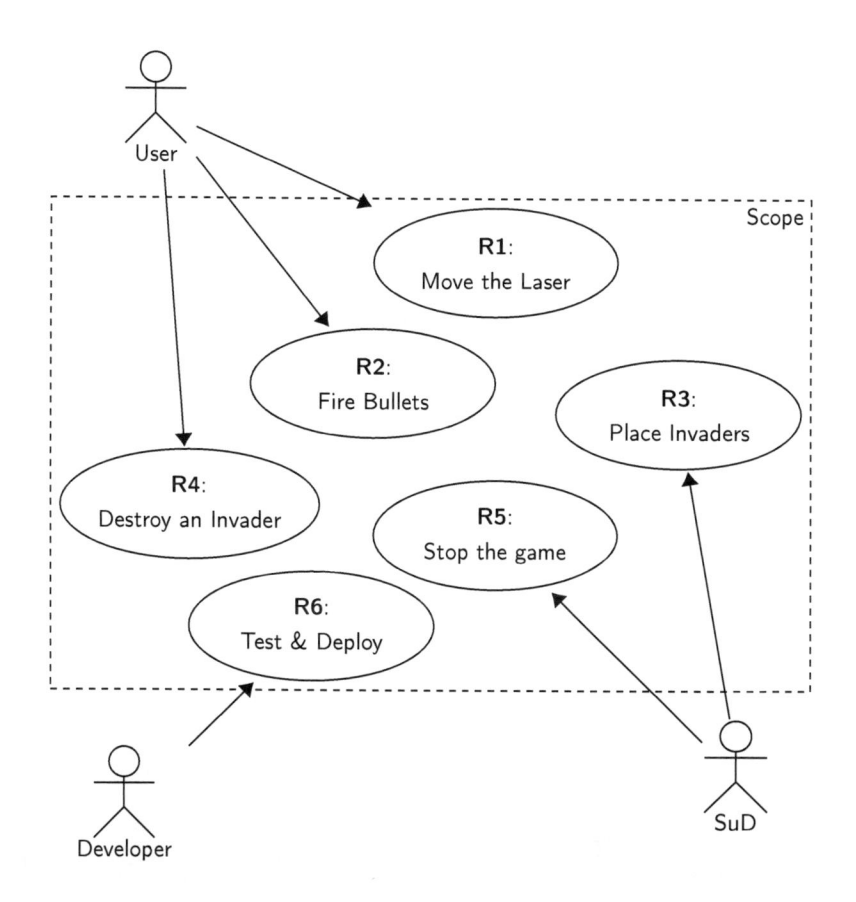

Figure 4.10: UML Use Case Diagram of Space Invaders, Updated

What else does the traceability matrix tells us? It makes it visually obvious that three columns are still "check mark free": `R2`, `R4`, and `R5`. These requirements are still not implemented.

Large projects will definitely need such a matrix to be created during the design phase when the architecture is developed. There could be multiple matrices, or if you use some software to manage them, they can be multi-dimensional. The goal is to connect elements of different processes: requirements analysis, design, architecture, implementation, testing, and so on. Each of

183

them has their own decomposition of the scope: by objects, by test cases, by requirements, by components, by files, by people, and so on. Traceability matrices help us understand whether they are all interlinked.

Now let's implement the requirement `R2` to let the User fire Bullets. The implementation of the `bullet` will be very similar to the one we have for `invader`:

```
function bullet(w) {
  return {
    window: w,
    launch: function(x) {
      const div = this.window.document
        .createElement('div');
      div.id = 'bullet';
      div.style.left = x + 'px';
      this.window.document.getElementById('field')
        .appendChild(div);
      this.fly(-5);
    },
    fly: function(dy) {
      const div = this.window.document
        .getElementById('bullet');
      const rect = div.getBoundingClientRect();
      const y = rect.top + dy;
      if (y < 0) {
        div.remove();
      } else {
        div.style.top = y + 'px';
        this.window.setTimeout(function() {
          this.fly(dy);
        }.bind(this), 10);
      }
    },
  };
}
```

The Bullet flies using the `setTimeout()` clock-watcher, just like it was done for `invader`. The only important difference is that it removes the `div` from the HTML once it flies too high and the `y` is getting smaller than zero. This is how we modify the code of the `laser`:

```
shoot: function() {
  const b = bullet(this.window);
  b.launch(this.x());
},
init: function() {
  this.window.addEventListener('keydown', function(evt) {
    // ...
    if (evt.keyCode === 32) {
      this.shoot();
    }
  }.bind(this));
},
```

Everything works just fine, but if you open it in your browser and hit ⬜ a few times, you will see a weird behavior of the Bullet. It speeds up every time you hit the button. This happens because the Laser doesn't make the Bullet unique. It creates and launches new Bullets every time the button is hit. We don't want this. Let's fix it by encapsulating the Bullet inside the Laser, just like our architecture was initially designed:

```
function laser(w) {
  return {
    window: w,
    bullet: bullet(w),
    shoot: function() {
      if (!this.bullet.flying()) {
        this.bullet.launch(this.x());
      }
    },
    init: function() {
      this.window.addEventListener(
        'keydown', function(evt) {
          // ...
          if (evt.keyCode === 32) {
            this.shoot();
          }
        }.bind(this)
      );
    },
  };
}
```

Before launching the Bullet, we check whether it's flying now using a new method `flying()`, which is implemented like this:

```
function bullet(w) {
  return {
    flying: function() {
      return this.window.document
        .getElementById('bullet') != null;
    },
  };
}
```

This seems like a good solution, but some programmers may criticize me for using this solution instead of a well-known Observer *design pattern*. The story behind this is simple: many years ago, most advanced programmers realized that the code they write in different projects have a lot in common. Spending time in each project to decide the right design is redundant if we can just reuse what was created in previous projects. Some of them even decided to create a catalog of design solutions and publish them. That's how design patterns were born.

Many people criticize design patterns and people who use them for their lack of imagination and the tendency to use a hammer for everything they see around them, even though it's not a nail. This criticism does make sense: design patterns are not supposed to replace programmers. Their intent is to help programmers understand what our ancestors have already solved and what their solutions look like. Using this knowledge, we may create even better solutions, or just copy what they've done; the choice is ours. But without knowing the catalog of patterns, there is no choice—we always re-write everything from scratch, making the same mistakes they've made dozens of years ago.

The Observer pattern is applicable when we have a "subject" object (the Bullet that flies) and an "observer" object, which is interested in knowing when the Bullet will fly out of the screen or maybe hit the target. The observer must inform the subject that it is interested in getting notifications, and the subject must remember it and notify the observer when something important happens. Let's redesign our `bullet` to implement the Observer design pattern:

```
function bullet(w) {
  return {
    launch: function(laser, x) {
      // ...
      this.fly(laser, -5);
    },
    fly: function(laser, dy) {
      // ...
      if (y < 0) {
        div.remove();
        laser.missed(); // Here!
      } else {
        // ...
      }
    },
  };
}
```

Now, the method `launch()` expects two arguments. The first one is the observer, which is the `laser`. The Bullet launches, flies, and when it hits something, it calls `laser.hit()` to inform the `laser` that the mission is complete. Here is what happens in the `laser`:

```
function laser(w) {
  return {
    bullet: bullet(w),
    loaded: true,
    shoot: function() {
      if (this.loaded) {
        this.loaded = false;
        this.bullet.launch(this, this.x());
      }
    },
    missed: function() {
      this.loaded = true;
    },
    init: function() {
      this.window.addEventListener(
        'keydown', function(evt) {
          // ...
          if (evt.keyCode === 32) {
            this.shoot();
          }
        }.bind(this)
      );
    },
  };
}
```

When the Laser is created, it's attribute `loaded` is `true`. When the Bullet is fired, the attribute `loaded` is set to `false`, and stays like that until the method `missed()` is called by the `bullet`.

This design may look a bit more complex than the one we had before, but it is more powerful and we will see it very soon when we start killing Invaders.

★
Update the Glossary and the text of the Requirements to reflect the changes made above.

★ ★

Name five other design patterns and explain how they work.

★ ★

Suggest a different set of names for our objects, instead of `field`, `army`, `invader`, `laser`, and `bullet`.

★ ★

Read my blog post: *Design Patterns and Anti-Patterns, Love and Hate (2016)*.

4.9 Decorators

Now is the time for my favorite OOP practice that makes OOP truly shine and impress us programmers if we do it right: *decorators*! There are two ways to add functionality to an existing object: 1) modify its code, making it larger; or 2) create a decorator that will add the functionality and encapsulate the original object. The second option is preferable for an obvious reason: we don't want our objects to become larger every time we need to add functionality to the system. Instead of explaining to you what decorators are, I will demonstrate by example.

In our code, we have very similar pieces of functionality that move DOM elements either left-to-right (the Laser and Invaders) or bottom-to-top (the flying Bullet). This code is duplicated three times in three objects (with very slight modifications):

```
const div = this.window.document.getElementById('bullet');
const rect = div.getBoundingClientRect();
const y = rect.top + dy;
div.style.top = y + 'px';
```

Here we get the element from the DOM, get its bounding rectangle, read the vertical y coordinate, and then save back a modified value of it. These manipulations move the element vertically by `dy` pixels. The Laser is moved left and right; the Bullet flies up straight; and Invaders move left, right, and down. Obviously, the functionality is very similar and the code is duplicated, which is a threat to maintainability and an obvious sign of bad coding style. To get rid of the duplication, we may introduce a new *utility object* (an object outside of our object diagram) `div`, to centralize all operations with DOM `<div>` elements:

```
function div(w, i) {
  return {
    window: w,
    id: i,
    rect: function() {
      return this.element().getBoundingClientRect();
    },
    element: function() {
      return this.window.document.getElementById(this.id);
    },
    move: function(v) {
      const rect = this.rect();
      const x = rect.left + v.dx;
      const y = rect.top + v.dy;
      const div = this.element();
      div.style.left = x + 'px';
      div.style.top = y + 'px';
      return v;
    },
  };
}
```

The method `move()` is universal and can be used by the `laser`, the `bullet`, and anyone else, including tests. In order to move any DOM element, we need to make an instance of `div` and ask it to move the element:

```
const d = div(window, 'bullet');
d.move(vector(+15, 0)); // Move right by 15px
```

The `div` uses another utility object of type `vector` (the argument `v` of the method `move()`), which is defined like this:

```
function vector(x, y) {
  return {
    dx: x,
    dy: y,
  };
}
```

This object is the most primitive one of anything we've seen before; it doesn't have any methods. Some programmers may call it a *data object* or a *data transfer object* (frequently referred to as DTO). Many OOP enthusiasts will tell you that having DTOs in your code is an immediate indicator of procedural programming. Instead of encapsulating the data and creating methods to work with them, we let anyone read and write our attributes `dx` and `dy`. They would be right and I fully support this principle: no data objects in our OOP code! However, the primitive object `vector` is not really an object, but rather a *data structure* provided by JavaScript to help us transfer a bit more complex blocks of data than simple integers and strings. A vector is a *hash map*, which is one of the basic data structures used in programming.

Long time ago, the so-called "von Neumann architecture" introduced by John von Neumann in 1945, started to dictate the principles of software engineering for programming language designers. The architecture suggested a clear separation between the memory of a computer and its instructions. First programming languages like ALGOL, FORTRAN, and COBOL, were designed to let programmers manipulate the data through statements and operators. Those languages also had *procedures*, which were creatures very similar to what we call methods and functions nowadays. Composite data structures (arrays, structs, maps, etc.) and procedures together made the development of very large pieces of software possible. However, the readability and maintainability of them were very low. The key problem, in my opinion, was the leakage of data semantic; each procedure was deciding for itself what each piece of data meant and how it was supposed to be used. Eventually, two procedures started to treat the same data differently and errors would become inevitable. Object-oriented programming was introduced to solve this problem by protecting the data from the dictatorship of procedures. In OOP, unlike procedural programming, the data (objects) were deciding what they meant and how they were supposed to be modified. This is what was called *encapsulation*.

An intensive usage of primitive data structures instead of objects will quickly turn your software into a procedural ALGOL-like program, and you will lose everything OOP gives you, including encapsulation, data hiding, polymorphism, and so on. You will get back to the traditional data-manipulating programming practices, and will never ever smile again. Be careful and stay away from data structures. Only very primitive, like the `vector` we use here, are OK. Anything larger than that must become objects and hide the data they contain behind the wall of methods protecting it.

Let's use the introduced `div` and modify the existing functionality of the `bullet`:

```
fly: function(laser, dy) {
  const d = div(this.window, 'bullet');
  d.move(vector(0, dy));
  if (/* the Bullet is still flying */) {
    this.window.setTimeout(function() {
      this.fly(laser, dy);
    }.bind(this), 10);
  } else {
    // Remove the <DIV> from DOM
  }
},
```

How do we implement this "the Bullet is still flying" check, which literally means checking for whether the Bullet is still within the borders of the screen? We can add this validation to the object `div`, which is a bad idea because the size of the object will increase; or we can *extend* it via *aggregation*:

```
function smart_div(d) {
  return {
    div: d,
    off_borders: function() {
      const element = this.div.element();
      const box = element.parentElement
        .getBoundingClientRect();
      const rect = this.div.rect();
      return rect.left > box.width - rect.width
        || rect.left < 0
        || rect.top > box.height - rect.height
        || rect.top < 0;
    },
  };
}
```

The new object `smart_div` aggregates the only object `div` and adds the `off_borders()` functionality to it. Normally, aggregation means putting together a number of objects and building new functionality on top of them all, but one object also works. This is how `bullet` would look:

```
fly: function(laser, dy) {
  const d = div(this.window, 'bullet');
  d.move(vector(0, dy));
  if (smart_div(d).off_borders()) {
    // Remove the <DIV> from DOM
  } else {
    this.window.setTimeout(function() {
      this.fly(laser, dy);
    }.bind(this), 10);
  }
},
```

Visually, aggregation looks like this:

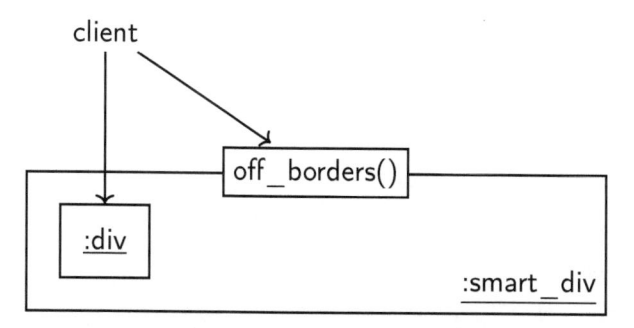

Figure 4.11: UML Object Diagram of Aggregation

The `smart_div` is not a `div`, but a new entity, with a new *interface*: the method `off_borders()`. Those who use it must know both interfaces, the `div` and the `smart_div`, and must understand how to interact with it. Moreover, the new object has to be constructed exactly where it is used. The client has to deal with two objects and must orchestrate the process; something is done by the `div`, while something else is done by the `smart_div`.

Aggregation is a great technique, but decorating is even better. A decorator is an aggregator, but it looks exactly like the object it aggregates. A decorator is a much more powerful tool than aggregation.

Consider an example: a list of students in a classroom. We decorate the list and make it contain only women. The new list is a decorator of the original one, but it behaves differently: there are only women in it. The user of the list doesn't have any idea about the fact that it's decorated. It uses the list just like any other list, for example, asking it: how many elements do you have? And the list requests the encapsulated list to return everybody, filters out men, and counts what's left. The result is returned to the requester. Then, we can decorate the list again and make sure the new list contains only students higher than 5.8'. The third decorator will encapsulate the second one, and also will have no idea where the second one gets the list of people. We can do it again and again, making the functionality more refined for the problem we need to solve every time:

```
UnderageStudents(
  StudentsWithExcellentGrades(
    OnlyTallStudents(
      OnlyFemaleStudents(
        AllStudents()
      )
    )
  )
)
```

In the end, it's still a list of students, just like the original `AllStudents` was. The users of the list won't have any idea what they deal with. For them, the structure of the object is invisible because the interface is still the same: every next *layer* of decorating exposes the same set of methods. This is what they call *polymorphism*, by the way.

Let's see how we can refactor our objects to make them utilize the power of OOP via decorators. The center of the design will be the object `div` that we will decorate with an object `patched` (notice the *arrow function expression*, which is a syntactically compact alternative to a regular function expression introduced in the 6th Edition of JavaScript in 2015):

```
function patched(d, ...ps) {
  return {
    div: d,
    patches: ps,
    move: function(v) {
      return this.patches.reduce(
          (a, p) => p.moved(this.div, a),
          this.div.move(v)
      );
    },
  };
}
```

The object `patched` encapsulates, like all decorators, the original object `div` and a list of "patches." Each patch is an object exposing a single method `moved()`. When the method `patched.move()` is called, it calls the method `move()` of the encapsulated `div`, and then sends the returned vector through all patches, asking them to correct the situation if necessary. Some of them may decide that the DOM element is too far away off the borders; some of them may decide that it's time to turn back and start moving to the other side; and so on. Each of them may do some manipulations with the `div`, and return a new `vector` to correct the direction of the movement. Visually, the design of `patched` looks like this:

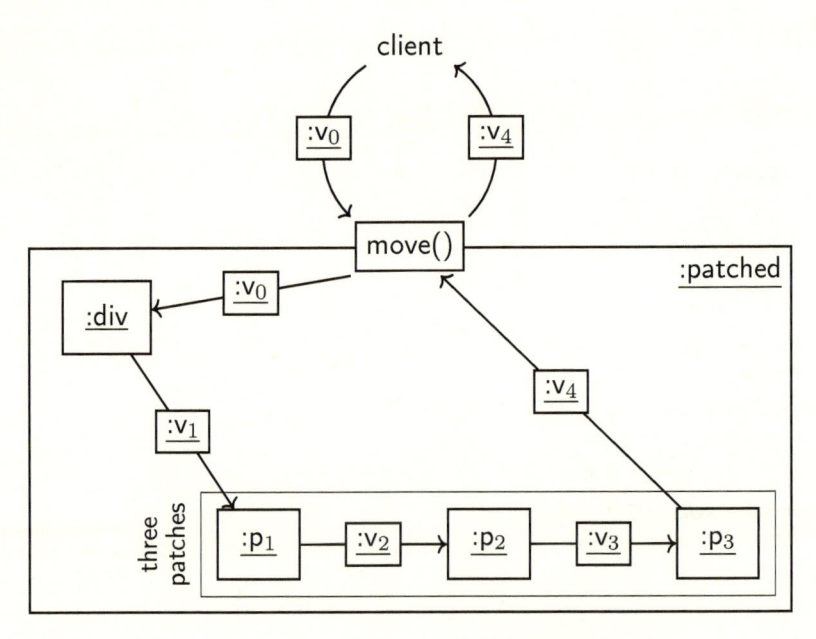

Figure 4.12: UML Object Diagram of `patched` Object

The client comes with `v₀` (the object `vector`), which contains the direction to move the `patched` object. The `div` makes the movement and returns a new vector `v₁` (or maybe the same one—it's up to the `div`). Then, the patch `p₁` analyzes the situation and makes some changes to the DOM, if necessary, and returns a new vector `v₂`, and so on until the last patch is done and the vector `v₄` (if there are three patches encapsulated) goes back to the client.

Let's say we want the `bullet` to destroy itself when it flies off the screen and inform the `laser` about it. We will need a set of four patches:

```
fly: function(laser, dy) {
  const v = patched(
    div(this.window, 'bullet'),
    outside((div, vector) => vector(0, 0)),
    missed(laser),
    trace(),
    grave()
  ).move(vector(0, dy));
  if (v.dy != 0) {
    this.window.setTimeout(function() {
      this.fly(laser, dy);
    }.bind(this), 10);
  }
},
```

The `outside` patch will check whether the DOM element is still inside the borders of its parent element (the `<field>`), and if it's not, it will call the encapsulated `action` and return what it returns:

```
function outside(a) {
  return {
    action: a,
    moved: function(div, vector) {
      const element = div.element();
      const box = element.parentElement
        .getBoundingClientRect();
      const rect = div.rect();
      let v = vector;
      if (rect.left > box.width - rect.width
        || rect.left < 0
        || rect.top > box.height - rect.height
        || rect.top < 0) {
        v = a(div, v);
      }
      return v;
    },
  };
}
```

The `missed` patch will also check whether the DOM element is still inside the borders of its parent element. If it's not, it will call the `missed()` method of the encapsulated `laser` (pay attention to the reuse of `outside` here in order to avoid code duplication, and not reimplement the borders checking functionality):

```
function missed(lz) {
  return {
    laser: lz,
    moved: function(div, vector) {
      const out = outside((d, v) => vector(0, 0));
      if (out.moved(div, vector).dy == 0) {
        lz.missed();
      }
      return vector;
    },
  };
}
```

The `trace` patch will simply print a supplementary message to the `console.log` in order to make testing and debugging simpler:

```
function trace() {
  return {
    moved: function(div, vector) {
      const rect = div.rect();
      console.log(
        'The div #' + div.id + ' moved to ' + rect.left +
        'x' + rect.top +
        ' with (' + vector.dx + ', ' + vector.dy + ')'
      );
      return vector;
    },
  };
}
```

The `grave` patch will remove the element from the DOM if the vector it receives is `(0,0)` vector:

```
function grave() {
  return {
    moved: function(div, vector) {
      if (vector.dx == 0 && vector.dy == 0) {
        div.element().remove();
      }
      return vector;
    },
  };
}
```

This is how our `laser` will use the new `div` with its decorator `patched` in the method `move()`:

```
move: function(dx) {
  patched(
    div(this.window, 'laser'),
    outside((d, v) => d.move(vector(-v.dx, v.dy))),
    trace()
  ).move(vector(dx, 0));
},
```

The logic is much simpler here; the `outside` will check whether the Laser is already outside of the field, and it will move it back.

And finally, here is the `attack()` of the `invader`:

```
attack: function(v, dx) {
  const after = patched(
    div(this.window, this.id),
    outside((div, vector) =>
      div.move(vector(vector.dx, 20))),
    outside((div, vector) =>
      vector(-vector.dx, vector.dy)),
    trace()
  ).move(vector(dx, 0));
  if (after.dx != 0) {
    this.window.setTimeout(function() {
      this.attack(v, after.dx);
    }.bind(this), v);
  }
},
```

Here, the patch `outside` is used twice. The first one moves the Invader down by 20 pixels, and the second one tells it to change the direction by returning a new vector with an inversed `dx`.

The `patched`, in the suggested design, is a decorator, while patches are *strategies* (this is yet another common name for the design we introduced). Every strategy can also be decorated, if necessary, and the `patched` itself can also be decorated when some new functionality is required.

★
Explain how `Array.reduce()` works in JavaScript.

★★
Make the Bullet fly with acceleration, increasing the speed every five steps forward.

★★
Remove the dots from the `...ps` in the declaration of object `patched` and make necessary changes in the code to make it work.

★★
Refactor the method `patched.move()` to get rid of the `reduce()`.

★★
Make the Invaders move a bit faster every time they shift down closer to the Laser.

★★
Explain SOLID principles.

★★
Name three other primitive data structures frequently used in programming, aside from the hash map mentioned above.

★ ★

Read my blog post: *Composable Decorators vs. Imperative Utility Methods (2015)*.

★ ★

Read my blog post: *Vertical and Horizontal Decorating (2015)*.

4.10 Boolean

You probably noticed pretty complex statements we used inside `if` and even as a result of `return`. For example, this one in `smart_div`:

```
return rect.left > box.width - rect.width
  || rect.left < 0
  || rect.top > box.height - rect.height
  || rect.top < 0;
```

This is called a *boolean expression*, which deals with boolean values instead of numbers and has its own operators, instead of addition and multiplication we used to have in arithmetic expressions. For example:

```
you_will_buy_coffee = you_are_thirsty AND
  (you_have_cash OR you_have_visa_card) AND
  (NOT the_cafe_is_closed)
```

Here `you_are_thirsty` and others are boolean operands while `AND`, `OR`, and `NOT` are the operators. The rest you can figure out yourself, I believe.

★
Why they are called "boolean"?

★ ★ ★
Study boolean algebra and prove that $\overline{a \wedge b} = \overline{a} \vee \overline{b}$.

4.11 IoC

Let's try to make the Bullet not only fly up, but also kill Invaders if it meets them. Let's start with the `bullet` and add a new patch to its set of patches that correct the behavior while it flies:

```
const v = patched(
  div(this.window, 'bullet'),
  kill(army), // Here!
  missed(laser),
  outside((div, vec) => vector(0, 0)),
  trace(),
  grave()
).move(vector(0, this.dy));
```

The new patch `kill` should look like this:

```
function kill(a) {
  return {
    army: a,
    moved: function(div, vector) {
      this.army.kill(div.rect().left, div.rect().top);
      return vector;
    },
  };
}
```

It encapsulates the `army` and on each move of the `bullet`, it asks the Army to make an attempt to kill some Invaders, which are located under the `(x,y)` position (the coordinates of the Bullet). The `army` does the work and destroys them, if they are there. Here is how the `army` will do it in its method `kill()` (I show the the entire object because there are many other changes):

```
function army(w) {
  return {
    window: w,
    invaders: [],
    total: 0,
    init: function(v = 10000) {
      this.launch(v);
    },
    kill: function(x, y) {
      this.invaders.forEach(function(i, idx, obj) {
        if (i.fire(x, y)) {
          obj.splice(idx, 1);
        }
      });
    },
    launch: function(v) {
      const i = invader(this.window, this.total++);
      this.invaders.push(i);
      i.launch();
      this.window.setTimeout(function() {
        this.launch(v - 50);
      }.bind(this), v);
    },
  };
}
```

The `army` now encapsulates the array of Invaders and removes some of them when they are killed. It calls method `fire` in each of them and if the method returns `true`—meaning the Invader was killed—it gets out of the array. Here is how the `invader` is modified:

```
function invader(w, i) {
  return {
    window: w,
    id: 'invader' + i,
    alive: true,
    fire: function(x, y) {
      const d = div(this.window, this.id);
      const r = d.rect();
      let killed = false;
      if (x < r.left + r.width && x > r.left
          && y < r.top + r.height && y > r.top) {
        this.alive = false;
        killed = true;
      }
      return killed;
    },
    attack: function(v, dx) {
      const after = patched(
        div(this.window, this.id),
        outside((div, vec) => div.move(vector(vec.dx, 20))),
        outside((div, vec) => vector(-vec.dx, vec.dy)),
        trace()
      ).move(vector(dx, 0));
      if (after.dx != 0 && this.alive) {
        this.window.setTimeout(function() {
          this.attack(v, after.dx);
        }.bind(this), v);
      }
      if (!this.alive) {
        div(this.window, this.id).element().remove();
      }
    },
  };
}
```

The newly introduced attribute `this.alive` is required in order to synchronize the object in a multi-threaded situation: the method `attack()` may be still in progress while the method `fire()` is called. The Invader may not destroy itself immediately in the method `fire()`. Instead, it has to set the flag signaling that the Invader is perfectly ready for dismissal. The interaction of four objects looks like this:

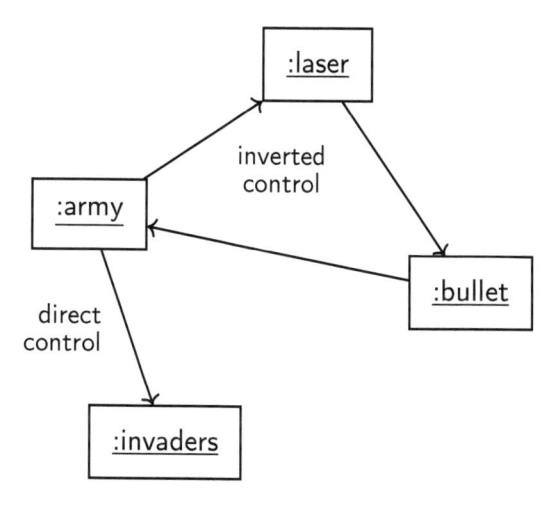

Figure 4.13: UML Object Diagram of Space Invaders

What happens between the `army` and `invaders` is the traditional *direct* flow of control. The `army` goes through the array of items, calls each of them, gives them some data, expects them to do certain things, and return the result of the execution.

What happens between three objects—the `army`, the `laser`, and the `bullet`—is an *inverted* scenario of events. The `army` is sent as an argument to the method `laser.init()`, and then to the method `bullet.launch()`. Then, when the Bullet moves, it calls the method `army.kill()`. The `army` doesn't know when it will be called. It doesn't control the flow of events. It's just being passively sent to another object and waits until that object decides to call it. This is why this design is called inversion of control (IoC). It's very popular in OOP mostly because it *decouples* objects, making them less dependent on each other.

Indeed, in the first scenario with the direct control, the `army` has to know exactly how `invaders` work. They will not be able to change their design without modifying the `army` too. In the second scenario, there is a bit more flexibility: the `army` can be passed to many other objects and they will all depend on its interface. Speaking honestly, I can't strongly vouch for any significant advantages of the inverted design. If the direct traditional design is done right, it would also be flexible and decoupled.

★
Who suggested the name IoC and when?

★
Explain exactly how the `Array.splice()` method works.

★ ★
Why I didn't use `this.invaders.length` as a counter of Invaders, but added `this.total`?

★ ★
Read my blog post: *How Does Inversion of Control Really Work? (2017).*

4.12 Immutability

Finally, let's implement the last requirement `R5` and stop the game when an Invader is too low. First, we create a new "patch" and name it `quit`:

```
function quit(a) {
  return {
    army: a,
    moved: function(div, vector) {
      const element = div.element();
      const box = element.parentElement
        .getBoundingClientRect();
      const rect = div.rect();
      if (rect.top > box.height - rect.height) {
        this.army.stop();
      }
      return vector;
    },
  };
}
```

Then, we add it to the Invader together with a new method `stop()`:

```
function invader(w, i) {
  return {
    // ...
    stop: function() {
      this.alive = false;
    },
    attack: function(army, v, dx) {
      const after = patched(
        div(this.window, this.id),
        outside((div, vec) => div.move(vector(vec.dx, 20))),
        outside((div, vec) => vector(-vec.dx, vec.dy)),
        quit(army),
        trace()
      ).move(vector(dx, 0));
      // ...
    },
  };
}
```

Now, the `army` will have to pass itself to `invader.launch()` to make it possible for the Invader to call it back, and ask to stop

209

the entire set of Invaders when one of them if too low. Here is the `army.stop()` method:

```
function army(w) {
  return {
    // ...
    stop: function() {
      this.invaders.forEach((i) => i.stop());
      alert('Game over!');
    },
    launch: function(v) {
      // ...
      i.launch(this);
      // ...
    },
  };
}
```

It seems that the game is implemented.

There's one last thing we have to discuss, and you'll be fully prepared to create your own object-oriented software. Take a look at the object `army` and its method `launch` one more time:

```
function army(w) {
  return {
    window: w,
    invaders: [],
    total: 0,
    launch: function(v) {
      const i = invader(this.window, this.total++);
      this.invaders.push(i);
      i.launch(this);
      this.window.setTimeout(function() {
        this.launch(v - 50);
      }.bind(this), v);
    },
  };
}
```

There are three attributes: `window`, `invaders`, and `total`.

What is the difference between them? Some programmers may tell you that `window` is *immutable*, while `total` is *mutable*. They will tell you this because we do `this.total++` and change the value of `this.total`, but never change the value (as they think) of `this.window`. Don't listen to them. All three attributes are equally mutable because we ask them to do something with the data they represent. The `this.windows` represents a large entity known as DOM, with kilobytes of data inside, while the `this.total` represents just a few bytes. However, what is the difference? There is no difference. They are both attributes pointing us to objects that represent data and other objects.

The question is whether the object `army` is mutable or immutable. Immutable objects never modify their attributes. In our example, a modification of an attribute would be something like this:

```
const a = army(window);
a.window = x;
```

In this example, we encapsulate `window` and then *inject* a new `x` into `a` instead of it. This modification makes the object mutable and it's absolutely bad practice. Aside from that, everything we've done in our application is perfectly valid, and all our objects are immutable.

★
Modify the code to show the score to the User when the game is over: the total amount of Invaders created during the game.

★ ★
The functionality of checking whether one `<div>` is inside another one is duplicated in a few places in the code. Refactor this by introducing a new method, `div.inside()`.

★ ★
Read my blog post: *Gradients of Immutability (2016)*.

★ ★ ★
Read *Object Thinking (2004)* by West [18].

Epilogue

This book is over, thanks for buying and reading it. I hope it's just a beginning of your tech career. You most definitely need to read *Elegant Objects* (a book series of mine), in order to truly understand object-oriented programming. You may also enjoy *Code Ahead* (yet another book series of mine), which explains software engineering and its discipline.

Also, to become a great software developer you will have to learn networking, machine learning, relational databases, NoSQL, XML, cloud computing, transactions, project management, and LaTeX (unfortunately, I didn't have time and space to touch any of these topics in this book).

I would also recommend you read my blog at www.yegor256.com.

The end.
Moscow, Russia
2019-2020

Designed in LaTeX

Bibliography

[1] Kent Beck. *Test-Driven Development*. Addison-Wesley Professional, 2003.

[2] Frederick P Brooks Jr. *The Mythical Man-Month*. Addison-Wesley Longman Publishing Co., Inc., 1995.

[3] Alistair Cockburn. *Writing Effective Use Cases*. Addison-Wesley Professional, 2000.

[4] Michael Feathers. *Working Effectively with Legacy Code*. Prentice Hall Professional, 2004.

[5] David Flanagan. *JavaScript: the Definitive Guide*. O'Reilly Media, Inc., 2006.

[6] Martin Fowler. *Refactoring: Improving the Design of Existing Code*. Addison-Wesley Professional, 2018.

[7] Steve Freeman and Nat Pryce. *Growing Object-Oriented Software, Guided by Tests*. Pearson Education, 2009.

[8] Brian Goetz et al. *Java Concurrency in Practice*. Pearson Education, 2006.

[9] Danny Goodman. *Dynamic HTML*. O'Reilly Media, Inc., 2002.

[10] Elliotte Rusty Harold, W Scott Means, and Katharina Udemadu. *XML in a Nutshell*. O'Reilly Sebastopol, 2004.

[11] Jez Humble and David Farley. *Continuous Delivery*. Pearson Education, 2010.

[12] Brian W Kernighan, Rob Pike, et al. *The UNIX Programming Environment*. Prentice-Hall Englewood Cliffs, 1984.

[13] Jon Loeliger and Matthew McCullough. *Version Control with Git*. O'Reilly Media, Inc., 2012.

[14] Robert C Martin. *Clean Code*. Pearson Education, 2009.

[15] Steve McConnell. *Code Complete*. Pearson Education, 2004.

[16] Glenford J Myers, Corey Sandler, and Tom Badgett. *The Art of Software Testing*. John Wiley & Sons, 2011.

[17] P Rita Mulcahy et al. *PMP exam prep*. RMC publications, 2009.

[18] David West. *Object Thinking*. Pearson Education, 2004.

[19] Karl Eugene Wiegers. *Peer Reviews in Software*. Addison-Wesley Boston, 2002.

[20] Karl Wiegers and Joy Beatty. *Software Requirements*. Pearson Education, 2013.

Index

`.eslintrc.json`, 127
`.gitignore`, 100
`DOCTYPE`, 152, 156
`Gruntfile.js`, 121
`Makefile`, 120, 124
`addEventListener()`, 152
`appendChild()`, 184
`assert`, 107
`bind()`, 174
`console`, 108, 109, 111, 200
`const`, 115
`describe()`, 112
`equal()`, 164
`getBoundingClientRect`, 152
`innerHTML`, 169
`it()`, 112
`keyCode`, 152
`let`, 115
`master`, 136
`node_modules`, 117
`onload`, 152
`package.json`, 116
`require()`, 115, 164
`return`, 83
`setTimeout()`, 174
`strictEqual()`, 112
`throw`, 91
`v()`, 152
`var`, 115

Berners-Lee, Tim, 27
CISC, 35
DSL, 115
ESLint, 126, 127, 143
GraalVM, 35
Homebrew, 117
LLVM, 35
MoSCoW, 136
Neumann, John von, 192
Nginx, 103
Nishikado, Tomohiro, 137
OCUP, 149
POSIX, 146
Plankalkül, 30
RISK, 35
SDLC, 133, 136
cpplint, 125
eXtreme Programming, 136

abbreviation, 156
abstraction, 36
administrator, 131
aggregation, 157, 194, 195
airport, 96, 98
ALGOL, 192, 193
algorithm, 128
altruism, 101
ambiguity, 142
Android, 120
anti-pattern, 107

Apple, 14, 15, 18
application, 101, 150, 158
    mobile, 120
architecture, 134, **145**, 150,
    155, 183, 185, 192
array, 114, 192
array function expression, 196
artifact, 130
Assembly, 32, 34, 35, 41, 44
association, 149
ASUS, 14, 15, 19
Atari, 137
attribute, 159, 162, 179, 206,
    210, 211
    protected, 154

backslash, 22
Badgett, Tom, 107
bandwidth, 97
Basic, 44
Beatty, Joy, 144
Beck, Kent, 107
bicycle, 15
binary, 25
bit, 26
boolean, 203
    algebra, 203
branch, **97**, 97, 102, 123
Brooks Jr, Frederick P, 149
browser, 153, 164, 173, 179, 185
    headless, 165
budget, 31
bug, 101, 106, 134
build, **120**, 122, 163, 166
    pipeline, 122, 131
    pre-flight, 122
    task, 122
byte, 26

C, 26
C++, 27, 125, 154
California, 18
car, 150

cardinality, 149
career, 132
certificate, 149
change request, 181
China, 18
Chromium, 103
Clean Code, 157
clock, 173
clone, 97
CMYK, 17
COBOL, 192
Cockburn, Alistair, 144
Code Complete, 55
code duplication, **168**, 169, 170,
    190, 199, 211
code review, 134
coding style, 125
cohesion, 111
command, 16, 21, 32
command line, 21
comment, 42
commit, 97, 98, 102, 106
    message, 99
    squash, 100
compilation, 34
compiler, 34
component, 100, 146, 180, 181
Composer, 120
composition, 157
concurrency, 173
confidence, 122
configuration, 165
consistency, 43
constructor, 162, 164
containerization, 132
content, 22
Continuous Delivery, 132
continuous delivery, 124
continuous integration, **123**,
    124, 148
contributor, 101
copy and paste, 114

coupling, 109, 111, 175
CPU, **15**, 18, 21, 32, 34, 35, 143, 146, 173
CSS, 147, 149, 171, 178, 179
cursor, 24
customer, 150, 151, 163, 181

data, 193, 210
data structure, 192, 193, 202
database, 97
debugging, 107, 176, 200
decorator, 190, **195**, 196, 201, 202
decoupling, 175, 207
Dell, 14, 15
dependency, 109, 114, 118, 121, 148, 165, **207**
    hell, 118
    injection, 109, 111
deployment, 18, 120, 130
design, 150, 155
design pattern, 186
DevOps, 132
DI container, 111
diagram
    activity, 149
    class, 148, 149
    component, 145
    deployment, 145, 147
    object, 145, 149, 190
    sequence, 154, 155, 173
    use case, 140, 141, 182
dictatorship, 192
directory, 21, 119, 120, 128
    current, 22
    home, 22
    root, 21
disclaimer, 119
disk, 143
Docker, 103
documentation, 41, 104, 105, 148

inline, 42
DOM, **152**, 162, 164, 166, 171, 172, 174, 179, 190, 191, 200, 210
donkey, 150
DRY, 170
DSL, 112
DTO, 192
Dynamic HTML, 32

ECMAScript, 131
email, 96
encapsulation, 190, **192**
end-user, 120
English, 28
ENIAC, 17
environment, 131, 147
    runtime, 33
estimate, 133
event, 156
exception, 106, 107, 111
expression, 203

Farley, David, 132
fear, 96, 107
Feathers, Michael, 171
feature, 31, 38, **97**, 106, 113, 123, 134, 150
feedback, 151
file, 32, 97, 119
    extension, 29, 95
    image, 130
    sound, 130
file system, 21
Firefox, 142, 165–167
flag, 206
Flanagan, David, 94
flexibility, 207
flow of control, 207
fork, 102
FORTRAN, 192
Fowler, Martin, 163
fragility, 122

framework, 112, 165, 175
Frankenstein's Monster, 150
FreeBSD, 19
Freeman, Steve, 167
fridge, 15
friend, 104
frustration, 102
function, **108**, 174, 196
    anonymous, 159, 172
functionality, 150, 163
future, 105

GHz, 34, 35
Git, **96**, 97, 116, 136
    push, 97
GitFlow, 100
GitHub, 47, 97, 102
glossary, 138, 139, 189
GNU, 120
Goetz, Brian, 180
gold platting, 181
Goodman, Danny, 32
Google, 127
Google Fonts, 31
GPU, 17
Growing Object-Oriented Software, Guided by Tests, 167
Grunt, 147, 163–165, 181
Gruntfile, 124

hacking, 39, 124
hardware, 15, 35, 124
Harold, Elliotte Rusty, 30
hash, 98, 100
hash map, 192, 202
HDD, 24
history, 96, 98
HTML, 32, 35, 36, 120, 147, **151**, 172, 178, 179, 184
HTML5, 36
HTTP, 167

Humble, Jez, 132

IDE, 31
IEEE, 144
image, 119
immutability, 210
inconsistency, 168
increment, 134
inheritance, 149, 157
initialization, 154
instruction, 33, 34, 96
Intel, 18
interface, 195, 207
Internet, 33, 137, 142
Internet Explorer, 142
interoperability, 142
interpreting, 32
inversion of control, 207
investor, 102
iOS, 120
IP, 167
IPC, 146
issue, 123
Istanbul, 128
iteration, 137, 143

Java, 107, 111, 113, 120, 154, 177
Java Concurrency in Practice, 180
JavaScript, 27, 108, 113, 120, 123, 140, 147, 157, 175, 196
JavaScript: the Definitive Guide, 94
JetBrains, 31
job interview, 25
JSON, 123

Karma, 165–167
Kernighan, Brian W, 20

label, 117

220

language, **27**, 36, 139
laptop, 20, 96–98
learning curve, 112
Lenovo, 14, 15, 18, 19
LG, 18
library, 101, 114, 175
    static and shared, 115
license, 119, 120, 124
lifecycle, 133, 137
line of code, 101
lines of code, 25, 35
linter, 125
Linux, 19, 101
listener, 173
locking, 176, 177
Loeliger, Jon, 100

MacBook, 14, 15, 18, 19, 30
macOS, 18
maintainability, 38, 125, 142, 168, 190
Make, 120
map, 192
Mark I, 17
Martin, Robert C, 157
Maven, 120
McConnell, Steve, 55
McCullough, Matthew, 100
Means, W Scott, 30
memory, 128
merge, 98, 134
    conflict, 98
merge request, 134
method, 104, 192
    builder, 170
    interception, 108
    manipulator, 170
    utility, 202
metrics, 130
Microsoft, 19
Microsoft Inc., 18
MIT, 119

Mocha, 112, 113, 115, 116, 122, 130
mocking, 109, 110, 164
module, 27, 100–102
MP4, 38
MSF, 136
multi-threading, 173, 206
mutation coverage, 130
Myers, Glenford J, 107

Node.js, 111, 112, 116
Npm, 116, 121, 124
number, 25
    floating point, 27

object, 145, 158, 180, 190, 193
    data, 192
    fake, 110
    mock, 109
    primitive, 192
    utility, 190, 192
object decomposition, 145
Object Thinking, 212
Observer, 187
OMG, 149
open source, 99, **100**, 101, 103, 124
operand, 203
operating system, 14, 18, 20, 25
operation
    arithmetic, 27
operator, 96, 203
output, 104

package, 100, 117, 120, 130
package manager, 116, 118, 121, 128
path, 21, 24
Peer Reviews in Software, 136
performance, 143
petabyte, 26
PHP, 120
Pike, Rob, 20

pipeline, 122
pixel, 16, 32, 37
planning, 133
plastic, 15
PMP exam prep, 136
polymorphism, 196
procedure, 192
product, 150
product statement, 139
production, 132
program, 25, 95
programmer, 96
programming
    object-oriented, 192
    procedural, 192
project, 96
promise, 180
Pryce, Nat, 167
pull, 98, 102
pull request, 102, 123
push, 98, 102
Python, 27

quality, 130, 133, 134

race condition, 175, 176
Rake, 120
RAM, 17
re-use, 114
readability, 124
recursion, 174
redundancy, 39, 43
refactoring, 163, 196
Refactoring: Improving the Design of Existing Code, 163
register, 34
release, 36, 114, 116, 130, 134, 150
    pipeline, 134
rendering, 36
repository, 97, 98, 102, 106, 116, 119, 120, 123

monolithic, 167
requirements, 133, 138, 140, 150, 180, 183, 189
    functional, 142
    non-functional, 142
resolution, 17
responsibility, 142
reverse engineering, 149
revert, 100
RGB, 17
risks, 133
Rita Mulcahy, P, 136
ROM, 17
Rubocop, 125
Ruby, 27, 101, 103, 112, 113, 115, 120, 125
Ruby on Rails, 112, 115
runtime, 146
RUP, 135, 136

Safari, **23**, 23, 32, 38, 129, 148, 163, 164
safety net, 122
salary, 39
Sandler, Corey, 107
scope, 133, 141, 181, 183
screen, 15, 36
SDD, 24
security, 102
semantic versioning, 117
semantics, 119, 192
server, 97, 120, 123, 132
side effect, 110
signal, 206
silicon, 15
soft skills, 144
software, 15, 18
software engineering, 150, 192
Software Requirements, 144
SOLID, 202
sorting, 114
South Korea, 18

Space Invaders, 137
spreadsheet, 31
Spring, 112, 113
SQL, 27
stakeholder, 133
statement, 96, 203
static, 146
static analysis, 125
steel, 15
strategy, 202
struct, 192
stub, 111
student, 196
stylesheet, 147
sub-directory, 21
Subversion, 99
SuD, 140
SWEBOK, 136
synchronization, 177, 206
system, 141

TCP, 165, 167
TDD, 107
team, 96
tech stack, 113
Terminal, 20
test, 105, 107, 120
    automated, 106
    case, 111
    coverage, 107, **128**
    fixture, 167
    integration, 107, 122, **164**, 168
    scaffolding, 167
    suite, 106
    unit, 163, 164
Test-Driven Development, 107
tester, 134, 181
testing, 34, 107, 119, 120, 134, 163, 165, 168, 176, 191, 200
TextEdit, 30

The Art of Software Testing, 107
The Mythical Man-Month, 149
The UNIX Programming Environment, 20
thread, 154, 173, 175, 176
thread-safety, 177
Tinder, 144
tool, 114
Torvalds, Linus, 102
touch typing, 25
Toyota, 163
traceability matrix, 180, 183
triple constraint, 133
trunk, 97, 123

Udemadu, Katharina, 30
UML, 134, 145–147, 149
underscore, 148
unit test, 176
Unix, 24
user story, 144

validation and verification, 136
variable
    global, 158, 159, 163, 164
VCS, 96, 99, 134
    centralized, 99
    decentralized, 97
vector, 193
venture capital, 102
version, 97, 114, 116, 131
Version Control with Git, 100
volunteer, 101, 102

watch, 15
Waterfall, 135
WebStorm, 31
West, David, 212
Wiegers, Karl, 144
Wiegers, Karl Eugene, 136
Windows, 14, 18, 19

Working Effectively with Legacy Code, 171
Writing Effective Use Cases, 144

x86, 17

XML, 123
XML in a Nutshell, 30

Z1, 17
ZIP, 96

Made in the USA
Middletown, DE
11 May 2024